Dr Marty Becker

Dr Marty Becker is the popular veterinary contributor to ABC-TV's *Good Morning, America*. He is also the author of two highly regarded US newspaper columns. In association with the American Animal Hospital Association, he hosts a nationally syndicated radio program.

Marty is an adjunct professor at both the Washington State University College of Veterinary Medicine, and at the Colorado State University College of Veterinary Medicine. Additionally, he has lectured at every veterinary school in the United States and has been named Companion Animal Veterinarian of the Year by the Delta Society and the American Veterinary Medical Association.

Marty is coauthor of the fastest-selling pet book in history, *Chicken Soup for the Pet Lover's Soul*.

Marty devotes his life to his family, which includes his beloved wife, Teresa, daughter, Mikkel, and son, Lex, along with all the furry family members on the Beckers' ranch in northern Idaho.

Gina Spadafori

Gina Spadafori has been blessed with the opportunity to combine two of her dearest loves – animals and words – into a career writing about animals. Since 1984, she has written an award-winning weekly column on pets and their care, which now appears in newspapers across the United States and Canada.

Gina has served on the boards of directors of both the Cat Writers Association and the Dog Writers Association of America. She has won the DWAA's Maxwell Medallion for the best newspaper column, and her column has also been honored with a certificate of excellence by the CWA. The first edition of her top-selling book *Dogs for Dummies* was given the President's Award for the best writing on dogs and the Maxwell Medallion for the best general reference work, both by the DWAA.

Along with coauthor Dr Paul D. Pion, a top veterinary cardiologist, she was given the CWA's awards for the best work on feline nutrition, best work on feline behavior and best work on responsible cat care for the top-selling *Cats for Dummies*. Gina lives in northern California in a decidedly multi-species home.

Do Cats Always Land on Their Feet?

101 of the Most Perplexing Questions Answered About Feline Unfathomables, Medical Mysteries & Befuddling Behaviors

MARTY BECKER, DVM
GINA SPADAFORI

An Orion paperback

This paperback edition first published in Great Britain in 2007
by Orion Books Ltd,
Orion House, 5 Upper St Martin's Lane,
London WC2H 9EA

10 9 8 7 6 5 4 3 2 1

A CIP catalogue record for this book
is available from the British Library.

ISBN 978-0-7528-8250-5

Printed and bound in Great Britain by
Mackays of Chatham, Kent

The Orion Publishing Group's policy is to use papers
that are natural, renewable and recyclable products and
made from wood grown in sustainable forests. The logging
and manufacturing processes are expected to conform to
the environmental regulations of the country of origin.

www.orionbooks.co.uk

Contents

Foreword

You don't have to know much about cats to know they're among the best companions you can have. But the more you know, the more you'll enjoy their company. (You can forget ever fathoming cats completely. You have a better shot at understanding the tax laws.)

I know this firsthand, because I've been living with an idiosyncratic cat for nearly thirty years. A flabby, crabby, lazy, lasagne-loving cat.

That cat, of course, is Garfield.

So many years with such a famous feline hasn't lessened my curiosity to find out more about all cats. And I know that all cat lovers find their pets mysterious (and often mischievous), and have questions both serious and not so serious to which they'd like some answers.

You can start anywhere when it comes to feline mysteries. For instance, 'Do cats always land on their feet?'

I won't spoil things by telling you the answer; turn a few pages for that. But I love that this most common of cat conundrums is the title of this delightful new book from a dream team: America's favorite veterinarian and his writing partner, who is also an award-winning pet-care journalist. Dr Marty Becker and Gina Spadafori love animals, and they also love sharing the answers to all those questions we cat lovers wonder about. The result is a book that's both educational and extremely entertaining.

You can even find out if lasagne is good for cats. I can tell you this: Garfield wholly approves of the answer!

Jim Davis, creator of 'Garfield'
www.garfield.com

Introduction
How well do you know your cat?

If you're like many cat lovers, the honest answer is not very well. In some ways, that air of mystery is part of this popular pet's appeal. You can love your cat, admire the furball as she sits like a perfect Victorian postcard on your windowsill, play with your cat and have long, heartfelt discussions with your cat – during which your cat will never disagree – but you can never really know what your cat is thinking.

Or can you?

While we humans pride ourselves on our ability to communicate verbally, our cats can read our every move. They are experts when it comes to deciphering body language and the tone of our voices. And they pay attention, because they want to know us better. The key to a closer and more enjoyable relationship with any animal is to return the favor: to understand them better and know more about what makes them tick.

Cats are not people, but we often treat them as if they are. When they act like cats – scratching furniture, marking their territory, hacking up a hairball – we sometimes are surprised. But we shouldn't be. Much of the feline behavior that seems strange to us two-leggers makes perfect sense if you're a cat. And if we humans could do some of the things cats do – such as see in near total darkness, give a race horse a run for its money, right ourselves in midair for a perfect four-point landing or lick every square inch of our bodies – we'd be superheroes.

So, do cats really always land on their feet? Is it true that not all of them love catnip . . . or milk? Were cats really once thought of as gods? The answers may surprise you, and we guarantee you'll find them interesting. Take a crash course in Feline 101, and you'll not only understand your cat better, you'll know her at a richer, deeper level – which means you'll be able to love her even more.

Dr Marty Becker and Gina Spadafori

Q Do cats always land on their feet?

A Not always. But they'll sure try. Cats are the perfect small predator, just as comfortable stalking a squirrel from tree to tree as they are chasing a wiggly piece of ribbon across the carpet. They've evolved with some nifty high-rise survival skills, including the ability to grab onto a branch with retractable crampons if they lose their footing. And if that doesn't work, they have that awe-inspiring ability to right themselves in midair so they can stick a perfect four-point landing.

This nifty feat would put any Olympic gymnast to shame. A falling cat will instinctively try to right himself from head to tail, first rotating his head into the proper position (to spot the ground just like all those crazy acrobats do on skis, snowboards, bikes or skateboards) and then sequentially spiraling the rest of his body so all his feet are oriented to the ground. As the body gains the right position, the cat will spread his legs in a sort of flying-squirrel fashion and relax his muscles in anticipation of landing. Spreading the impact over four points is considerably better than hitting on one, and a cat's cushy joints enable him to absorb a lot more impact than we mere humans can.

A cat's ability to rotate in midair isn't a foolproof strategy for surviving the perils of modern living, however. Veterinarians have long noted and studied what's called high-rise syndrome – the tendency cats have of being better able to survive falls from greater heights than lower ones. The most dangerous falls are from between two and six stories. Amazingly enough, a few urban cats have survived falls of up to thirty stories, albeit with severe injuries – broken legs and jaws, and collapsed lungs.

The difference may well be the cat's ability to set himself up for the best possible landing, in the way that all cats have been doing for generations. You see, that 'rotate and relax' maneuver takes time to implement. From the lower floors, it's thought a cat hasn't enough time to prepare himself for impact by getting himself in proper landing position. From the highest floors, the fall's too great to survive. In between, however, is a margin of survivability for the cat who lands on his feet.

Urban veterinarians say they start seeing cats who've fallen out of windows and off balconies in the spring, when people are anxious to enjoy the nice weather and open their windows. Cats aren't stupid, but it's really not in their nature to understand the implications of being twenty stories up. They don't think about it, and go about their business as always. Some cats simply lose their footing walking on a narrow balcony railing, while others jump after a moving object such as a bird. Hundreds of cats are killed or injured each year in falls.

It's best not to test a cat's ability to land on his feet. The answer is an easy one: Buy screens! That way, the cat can't get out easily and the bugs can't get in.

Q Which is the most popular pet in America, dogs or cats?

A In the mid-1980s, cats supplanted dogs as everyone's best friend, and the gap has grown steadily wider ever since. The most recent numbers say there are 90.5 million pet cats in the United States and Canada, and 73.9 million pet dogs. (In all fairness to dogs, though, cat lovers tend to have more than one cat. So more households – 43.5 million – have dogs, while 37.7 million households have cats.) Once upon a time, dogs far outnumbered cats in the fur-family department, but they had a head start. Early humans were hunters, and so were early dogs. We used them to help us detect, pursue and bring down game. And we shared the result – roast beast – with them.

It wasn't until we started farming and storing grain for the winter or lean years that we came to realize the value of cats – smaller predators who specialize in making life miserable and death quick for the kind of animals who eat that stored grain. More than a few people came to love cats as companions, but mostly they were kept around because of their skills at killing rodents.

Fast forward a few centuries.

We're not home as much as we were even a generation ago, and the homes we live in may be condos or apartments, or smaller houses built on smaller lots. While it's possible to keep a dog in all kinds of environments, they don't do well left alone, and they need more exercise and training than many of us can offer.

Guess which pet is perfectly suited to this modern lifestyle? With Mice-A-Roni seldom on the menu these days, cats are happy to fit into our busy lives and are delighted to share the time we have for them. They don't need to be walked, are happy to use a litter box (as long as it's clean) and sleep most of the time anyway.

Will they maintain their popularity? Probably. Although small dogs have become exceptionally popular in recent years – no doubt for the same reasons that have put cats on top – the beauty, grace and quiet companionship of cats suggests they'll not be giving up their crown as America's top pet any time soon.

Q Were cats once really worshipped as gods?

A Are you kidding? Cats are still worshipped. Just ask them!

Historically speaking, though, cats have figured prominently in the religions of Egypt, the Norse countries, and various parts of Asia. The Egyptians worshipped a goddess named Bast with the body of a woman and the head of a cat. Thousands of cat mummies have been discovered in Egypt, and ancient Egyptians even shaved their eyebrows in mourning when the family cat died.

In Siam (today's Thailand), the cat was so revered that a cat always rode in a chariot at the head of a parade celebrating the new king.

In Norse mythology, Freya, the most renowned and desirable of the goddesses, traveled around in a chariot pulled by cats.

Which is not to say cats were considered such a good thing everywhere and all the time. In the Middle Ages, cats were thought to be linked to the devil, and many an innocent cat was killed along with those people likewise thought to have connections to demons and witchcraft.

In the end, though, cats proved their worth and gained plenty of followers. Having turned from mouser to moocher, few cats these days are expected to earn their keep, and yet we keep them anyway. To be born retired: What is that, if not worship?

THE HEALING POWER OF FELINE FECES

Yes, the ancient Romans believed feline feces had healing powers. But they also thought drinking cups made of lead were a great idea, so the resulting brain damage may help explain it somewhat.

The Romans used a concoction of honey, cat dung, spices and fat to heal burns and wounds (just imagine how that smelled!).

Many cultures have used almost everything in, on or from cats in medicine. Even today, tiger parts are used in traditional Chinese medicine to treat all sorts of ailments. As a result, there are only fifty South China tigers left.

As late as the Middle Ages, a few medicinal concoctions still called for cat poop. One mixed white wine with cat dung to treat dizziness, fever or seizures. An ointment made of cat feces was used both to treat baldness and as a depilatory.

Q Do cats really need us? Can't they just take care of themselves?

A Unquestionably, cats are easy keepers. But anyone who adopts a cat thinking that cats are like house-plants or pottery, only furrier, is in for a big surprise. Kittens and cats seek out and need attention and affection. They also need routine care to prevent a number of common ailments, from hairballs to ingrown nails. And they need us to keep their litter box clean. (If we don't, they will refuse to use it – with consequences no one will enjoy.)

To care for your cat well, you need a few basic supplies, a premium feline diet, a high level of preventive health care (vaccinations, parasite control, good oral hygiene) and a veterinarian you know well enough to ask the questions you need answers to if problems arise. Cats who take advantage of all nine lives and live them all as happy, healthy felines have owners who follow the mantra 'Healthy pets see their vets for twice yearly wellness visits'.

But it's more than just supplies and vet visits. Cats love us and seek our company. They want and need to play with us, to snuggle with us, to bond with us. The idea of cats being aloof is a myth. They just love us in feline ways, like teenagers, only hairier and they don't ask for the car.

Although cats do need our love and care, they are still low maintenance compared to a lot of other pets. Cats are wonderful pets for people who work long hours, people who aren't able to exercise a lot because of age, injury or lifestyle, and people who just want the easygoing companionship a cat can provide.

Cats are arguably the most easygoing and adaptable pets you can choose, but they do have their own special needs. Your responsibility is to protect your cat and provide her with the care and love she needs. In return, you'll have a beautiful, loving companion for many, many years. Your cat always keeps up her end of the bargain, so make sure you keep up yours.

Q When my neighbor moved, his cat kept escaping and running back to their old house, and I've heard other stories about cats doing that. Why would they run away?

A Cats are very territorial. They make themselves feel at home by making their home smell like themselves – rubbing their cheeks and flanks on items, scratching, or even urine-marking like a graffiti artist who substitutes good old cat pee for paint (the latter behavior being perfectly reasonable to a cat, if perfectly disgusting to a person). Take a cat off his home turf and he's going to feel anxious. Cats would rather stay pretty much where they are, for life.

We're not like cats in this respect. Cats are homebodies, while we humans are kinetic and upwardly mobile.

Cats find this behavior of ours confusing and distressing, to say the least. Some will deal with their anxiety by trying to get back to a place where everything seems to smell the way it should. Like E.T., they want to go home.

Many people who've moved short distances have had the experience of their cats heading back to the old place time and time again. It's a good way to get to know the people who live where you used to, if nothing else. Even more amazing, a few cats have accomplished the feat of finding the old homestead even if it's hundreds of miles away.

The determination cats show in getting home has led some people to believe that cats prefer places to people. The same belief prompts some people to leave their cats behind when they move, figuring that the animals are happier at the old house and hoping the new residents take them in. Unfortunately, that sort of thinking lands a lot of cats in the local animal shelter as strays.

Cats are very much bonded to their people and will happily go wherever their family goes – just as long as the cat's owner takes a few simple steps to help him settle into the new surroundings. For a few weeks after the move, keep the cat in a single room with a litter box, food, water, a scratching post and favorite toys. Just as it takes a child a while to adjust to a new school and neighborhood, cats take some time to socialize and harmonize with their new surroundings. When the cat seems comfortable, the territory can be gradually increased until it encompasses the whole house.

When the world finally smells right to a cat and all the dust settles, a cat will once again turn his attention to the people in his life.

If your cat is allowed outdoors, keep him strictly indoors for several months after a move so he can 'reset' his internal compass to your new home. Better yet, moving is a great time to convert an outdoor cat to an indoor lifestyle!

Q Can a cat really be happy living completely inside?

A Good, knowledgeable, well-intentioned people on both sides of this issue have strong opinions, that's for sure. Perhaps the best answer is this: Some cats can be happy living inside and some can't.

Anyone who has watched a cat track a grasshopper across the lawn or sleep in the sun on a warm patio would not be telling the truth if they didn't admit cats love exploring the outdoors. And many people believe that denying an animal access to the natural world is unnatural, even cruel.

On the other hand, cats who are free to roam annoy neighbors, kill furry little critters and birds, and generally don't live as long as indoor cats. They're hit by cars, crushed in automatic garage doors, killed by loose dogs, poisoned either accidentally or sometimes intentionally, and come in contact with many more infectious diseases courtesy of neighbor kitties, unvaccinated feral cats, and wild animals. More often than not, outdoor cats just disappear, leaving their owners to wonder forever about their fate. The truth is most of these cats don't end up in another home or lost; they end up dead.

When they're kept inside from kittenhood and provided with attention and lots of what zookeepers call 'environment enrichment' (translation: toys, perches, scratching posts and

11

climbing trees, food puzzles, and things to do), many cats live long and happy lives inside. This is especially true of cats who live in urban areas, where outside is simply not an option, and suburban cats whose environs are just too dangerous (and whose neighbors really don't want kitty pooping in their yard).

Converting a cat who has had free access to the outside to a total homebody can be very difficult, however, and many people give in to their cat's demands and open the door. (You can get tips on keeping kitty in and making her life happy at the Web site of the Indoor Cat Initiative of the Veterinary College at the Ohio State University, www.indoorcat.org.)

The trend toward keeping cats indoors has been growing to the point now where many shelters, rescue groups and reputable breeders absolutely refuse to place a cat with anyone who won't promise to keep the animal inside.

As with any other hot topic, compromises are possible. Cat fencing – tall, nearly invisible nylon mesh mounted on a traditional wooden fence – is widely available from a handful of manufacturers to keep your cat safe in your yard. Most people would never dream of simply letting their dog wander around the neighborhood at will; they keep Fido in a fenced yard. Why not do the same for Fluffy?

Another option is to build a small, simple screened porch for your cat. (Again, there are some commercial products available that make it easy.)

If nothing else works for you and your cat, you can at least minimize the risk by keeping your pet in at night. It won't keep the peace with your neighbors, but it will minimize to a small extent some of the other risks to which your outdoor cat is exposed. To get him reliably coming inside before dark, feed him his yummiest meal at that time – in the kitchen.

Q What is it about the way cats walk that always makes them look so elegant and smooth?

A If you've ever carefully watched dogs walk, you may have noticed that they alternate sides when they step. In other words, the front right paw steps forward at the same time the rear left paw does. Then the front left and rear right paws step out. Speed this up and it's known as a trot.

Cats move differently. They step with both left paws, then both right paws. Their natural gait, in other words, is what's known as a pace. (Only camels and giraffes have the same natural gait, although some horses are trained to race using the pace.)

One thing cats and dogs do have in common: They walk on their toes.

Most cats have five toes on their front paws, but only four of them hit the ground. The fifth toe is called a dewclaw and is found on the inside of the front paw. The dewclaw is the feline equivalent of our thumb, and it's used for grasping prey and climbing trees. A normal feline back paw, by the way, has four toes that are all called into service when walking.

Q *What exactly is a hairball?*

A Cats spend 30 percent of their waking hours grooming themselves – which seems like a lot, until you consider that they spend 70 percent of their day sleeping. Still, they are very fastidious animals. Their tool of choice is that raspy tongue, which can pull free lots of hair, especially if the cat is longhaired or has a lot of undercoat (the soft, downy hairs that lie close to the skin).

Swallowed hair is indigestible, even for cats, so when it's in a cat's stomach, it has two ways to go: down and out or up and out. When it comes up – to the accompaniment of that middle-of-the-night 'ack! ack!' serenade every cat lover knows so well – it's a hairball.

If you want to impress your friends, the scientific name for that gummy mass you step in on your way to the bathroom at 2 a.m. is trichobezoar. It is made up of the excess hair your cat swallowed, held together with a sticky mucus . . . but you knew that from cleaning it off your bare feet, didn't you?

Hacking up a hairball every now and then is normal and usually doesn't cause problems, but if you see anything else in the mix, take the cat and the hairball (the former in a carrier, the latter in a plastic bag or container) to your veterinarian. Likewise, if your cat is hacking without producing a hairball, the vet is waiting to see you. Chronic coughing can be a symptom of many health problems, from heartworms to heart disease to asthma. Occasionally, hairballs can cause an obstruction that will require veterinary attention.

The easiest and best way to prevent hairballs is to brush your cat frequently. The more dead hair you pull out on your brush, the less she will have to swallow when she grooms. Regular brushing is good for your cat and good for your furniture and rugs.

For cats who seem to have a chronic problem with hairballs, additional fiber in the diet may help. Special hairball-busting diets can be recommended by your veterinarian; milder cases may be resolved by adding a little canned pumpkin (not pumpkin-pie-filling mix) to a cat's wet food.

One caution: While over-the-counter hairball remedies are available, don't let your cat become so dependent on them that you're always giving her hairball remedy. And definitely work with your veterinarian while using them. Overuse of hairball remedies can inhibit your cat's ability to absorb some essential vitamins. That's why it's also a good idea not to give them to your cat just before or after she eats.

The enduring feline mystery we can't help you with: Why do cats always hurl hairballs either on the most expensive fabric or the most well-traveled hallways? The best we can say: If your tummy hurt, wouldn't you want sympathy from a loved one? It also makes for great drama. So go brush your drama queen.

Q *How many bones does a cat have?*

A It depends on the cat. Or, more precisely, on her tail and feet.

A long-tailed Siamese will have more vertebrae than a manx with no tail or a Japanese bobtail with just part of a tail. And a cat with extra toes – they're called polydactyl – will have extra bones too.

The range is usually between 230 and 250, with the average cat counting about 244 bones – if cats could or cared to count.

Any way you count it, the average cat has about 30 more bones than we do – and think about how much bigger we are than cats. No wonder they can lick behind their shoulders and sleep in a perfect circle!

COUNTING TOES IN KEY WEST

Any number of toes over the norm (usually an extra one or two, but occasionally as many as three or four) makes a cat polydactyl, which means 'many fingers.' These cats are also sometimes known as Hemingway cats.

That's because the famous writer Ernest Hemingway became a fan of these cats after being given a six-toed cat by a ship's captain. Legend has it that sailors once valued polydactyl cats for their extraordinary climbing and hunting abilities, and they became common on sailing ships.

Polydactylism is a dominant genetic trait, which means just one polydactyl parent is enough to make a litter of polydactyl kittens.

Descendants of Hemingway's cats remain popular tourist attractions at the author's former residence (now a museum or, dare we say, cat house) in Key West, Florida. About sixty cats share the grounds, and about half are polydactyl.

Q ## Why do cats' eyes shine at night?

A Cats' eyes are more sensitive to light than ours are, which means they can see a lot better in low light than we can – which is what you'd expect from a nocturnal animal. Even cats can't see in total darkness, but they can get pretty close. And one of the most visible (pardon the pun) ways they've adapted to low-light conditions is revealed in those glow-in-the-dark eyes.

The glow is actually light reflected back from a layer of special cells behind the retina, called the *tapetum lucidum*, which is Latin for 'luminescent tapestry.' (We love showing off our Latin, even if we had to look it up first!) The retina is the light-sensitive tissue lining the back of the eye. Its job is to convert light into electrical impulses that are sent to the brain. The job of the *tapetum lucidum* is to catch all the light that didn't enter the retina directly and reflect it back in, so every tiny bit of light can be processed.

Add in the fact that a cat's pupils can dilate to three times the size of ours and they also have a larger cornea (the eye's outermost lens), and you can see why a cat has no need for night-vision goggles. The bottom line: A cat can see in conditions that are more than five times less bright than what we require.

Perhaps this ability to hunt by night has contributed to the alley cat's claiming the award for one of the most successful predators in the animal kingdom.

Long before a cat ever was caught in the headlights, the ancient Egyptians had another theory for why the cat's eyes glow at night: They believed the eyes of a cat reflected the sun, even at night when it was hidden from humans.

Q Why do cats' eyes contract to a vertical slit?

A If cats wore sunglasses or didn't evolve into creatures who have the nighttime munchies, they probably would have round pupils like ours.

But they're nocturnal hunters and see well in very dim light. Just as we adjust our headlights from normal headlights to brights, a cat's eyes adjust to different lighting conditions. In the daytime, cats have precise control over the amount of light reaching their eyes. This enables them to gaze out the window and zero in on that errant squirrel in the tree or big bird on the feeder.

Having eyes that reduce the pupils to slits rather than tiny circles gives the cat greater and more accurate control in different types of lighting; this ability is particularly important in bright sunlight.

Vertical slits also have another advantage over horizontal slits. Because the cat's eyelids close at right angles to the vertical pupil, a cat can reduce the amount of light even further by bringing her eyelids closer and closer together. Similar to the shutter on a camera, this combination of the vertical slits of the pupils and the horizontal slits of the eyelids enables the cat to make the most delicate adjustments to accommodate different lighting. And these actions, in combination, protect the eyes better than sunglasses.

It's a perfect setup for a nighttime hunter who loves to bask in the daytime sun.

This adaptation sets the domestic cat apart from her majestic relative, the lion. Because the lion hunts by day, her pupils do not have the same sensitivity to light as the domestic cat's. The lion's eyes contract — like ours do — to tiny circles, not vertical slits.

Q Do cats dream?

A Cats definitely remember things – in fact, they have great memories – so it makes sense to believe they have the ability to dream, just as people do. After all, dreaming is a normal part of organizing and reorganizing memories. Kind of a subconscious filing system, you could say.

Like humans, cat have two kinds of sleep. The deeper kind is characterized by rapid eye movements, so it's known as REM sleep. We know humans dream during REM sleep. We also know that when cats twitch their limbs and even their whiskers while they're asleep, they are in feline REM sleep. So it's not a far fetch to believe cats are dreaming, too.

What are they dreaming about? We'll never know. But we suspect the mice are fat and on crutches, birds can't fly, nasty neighborhood kids are nowhere to be seen, dogs disappear on command, invading cats from other territories scat with a mere glance, the pantry is full, and they've got opposable thumbs and a new can opener.

Q *What percentage of a cat's day is spent, well, catnapping?*

A Predators always sleep more than animals who have to spend their days finding vegetation to munch. The extra nap time is one of the perks of being higher up on the food chain. If you're a lion, you can sleep most of your life away, and as long as someone gets up now and then to bring down a hoofed animal, all is well.

Domestic cats spend about 70 percent of their lives asleep. As you've probably guessed, most of those hours are spent in short snatches of sleep – catnaps, of course.

Q My husband is allergic to our cat. What should I do?

A Divorce him. Or have an indoor cat and an outdoor husband.

Not really. In fact, these sorts of conflicts come up all the time and they are never, ever easy to resolve. Even more difficult than having a mate who's allergic to cats is having a child who has developed such allergies. (Although studies now show exposure to pets in childhood may prevent allergies later in life.) A mate can choose to live with mild to moderate allergies, after all, but what parent would choose suffering for their child?

More people are more allergic to cats than to dogs, and cat allergies are often more severe, as well. For people with asthma, a severe reaction to a cat can be more than annoying – it can be life threatening.

Nobody's really sure why cats are such an allergy trigger, but one thing any allergist will tell you: The increase in the popularity of cats and the trend toward keeping them inside has meant more sneezing, wheezing and red eyes among cat lovers. It's estimated that 6 to 10 million Americans are allergic to cats, and a lot of them would rather cope than give up their pets.

Cat fur isn't what causes allergies, so finding a cat with little or no fur won't help much. A substance called Fel D1, found in cat saliva and urine and deposited on skin and fur when a cat grooms, is the source of the problem. This allergen becomes part of what's commonly called dander – flakes of skin, secretions and saliva that a cat spreads wherever he wanders and that become airborne as he's petted, jumps or shakes. You don't have to live with a cat to be exposed to dander: Studies have found the stuff everywhere, even in a doctor's waiting room.

While every family will have to come to the decision that's right for their specific circumstances, there are a few tricks that might make living with a cat and allergies more comfortable for all but the most severe allergy sufferers.

First, find an allergist who will work with the allergy sufferer and accept that finding a new home for the cat is the last alternative, not the first one. After all, people who are allergic to trees or grass can't rid their environment of these things; there are ways to work around them. Working with an allergist can help get all a person's allergies under control and may leave a little 'breathing room' for keeping a cat.

Second, compromise. Establishing the bedroom as a cat-free zone (some of you may prefer a husband-free zone) will let an allergy sufferer sleep in peace. While sleeping with a cat on the bed is one of many pleasures of living with a cat, keeping puss on the other side of the bedroom door may enable you to keep both your cat and your mate.

Third, keep the house clean. Choose smooth, easy-to-clean surfaces in your home – tile or hardwood rather than carpet – and give the person with allergies a break from vacuuming and dusting. Use a vacuum with a filter and damp cleaning cloths to keep dander from going airborne. HEPA air filters for rooms and for the central heat and air-conditioning system may also help.

Fourth, keep your pet clean. Studies show that rinsing your cat weekly in clear water can reduce dander levels. Obviously, this task should also go to the non-allergic members of the family, as should cleaning the litter box.

The long-term view offers a couple of promising solutions, one of which is, admittedly, controversial. The most promising is the possibility of a vaccine that will prevent cat allergies. News of such a product erupted in the late 1990s and has given hope to the many people who are, shall we say, itching for just such a drug. The vaccine doesn't exist yet, but it's probably just a matter of time before some company comes up with it.

Now the controversial idea: The prospect of a cat who is genetically engineered to be truly hypoallergenic has been in the news. But given that the price tag is expected to be in the thousands of dollars – not to mention the hue and cry from people who don't think pets should be genetically modified – it's a bit of an iffy prospect how big a splash such cats will make.

The amount of allergen any cat produces varies from animal to animal, although studies suggest that black cats and unneutered males cause more problems for allergy sufferers.

Is it safe to have a pet bird if you have a pet cat?

Safe for whom? If you have a massive hyacinth macaw (or even the more common blue-and-gold), your cat may be the one who's in the most danger.

In general, though, while many people successfully manage multi-species households, you must always be careful when you're mixing predators and prey. That's true when you have dogs and cats, and it's true when you have cats and birds or small pets such as rats, hamsters or lizards. The lion doesn't lay down with the lamb in the wild, and you should not expect your cat to consider your canary as his brother. Keep these pets safely apart.

Also consider the stress factor. Birds know that cats are predators and they are prey. Gerbils and hamsters know it too. It can be tough for tiny prey animals to see a deadly predator lurking about all the time — even if their cage is very, very secure.

Considering how dangerous cat bites can be, you should regard any time your cat gets his paws (and especially his teeth or claws) on a pet bird or rodent as a medical emergency, even if the smaller pet seems fine. At the very least, your little critter may need a course of antibiotics. Once prey animals such as birds seem sick, they're often too sick to be saved. Word to the wise.

Q What causes diabetes in cats?

A In the last few years veterinarians have noted with alarm an increase in diabetes in cats. The trend parallels that in humans and the reason is much the same: obesity. In other words, fat cats like Garfield and Heathcliff are funny in cartoons, but a worry in real life.

Here's why: Diabetes develops when the pancreas is unable to make enough insulin, a hormone that regulates the metabolism of glucose (blood sugar). The more fat there is available in the body, the less available and less effective is the insulin the pancreas does make. In cats, recent studies have also linked diabetes to high-carbohydrate diets.

A change to a low-carb, high-protein diet (jokingly referred to as the 'catkins diet'), along with a gradual return to normal weight, may be enough to control diabetes in some cats. In others, weight loss and a change in diet may be aided by medication to lower blood sugar. Other cats will need insulin shots and regular monitoring of their blood sugar, both of which can be done at home.

The problem with a cat who needs such treatment is often psychological – for the owner! Once the owner becomes comfortable with giving the cat injections and settles into a feeding routine, it is possible for a diabetic cat to live a happy, comfortable life.

In addition to working with a veterinarian to make sure a diabetic cat is properly managed, this is one time when the encouragement and support of other cat lovers can help. No pet malady we know of has as well established a support network as the one for feline diabetes. Start with the Feline Diabetes Web site (www.felinediabetes.com), founded and managed by a human physician after her own cat was diagnosed.

There's a lot of really awful pet health advice on the Internet, which is why nothing beats a working relationship with a good veterinarian. But now and then we run across a site that's just top notch. Feline Diabetes is one. (And if you're asking, www.Veterinary Partner.com, run by the Veterinary Information Network, is another.)

Q Is it true that crash diets are dangerous for fat cats?

A Are you concerned about your cat's waistline? You should be! Too much food along with too little exercise is doing for our pets exactly what it's doing for us: Making them fat. And with cats, just as with us humans, obesity all too often leads to diabetes, joint diseases, heart problems, increased risk of cancer, and other serious health and behavioral issues.

Which is why weight loss is important. But a crash diet for a cat can be a train wreck. If overweight cats lose weight too quickly, they can develop a serious liver disorder that can be challenging to treat and is occasionally fatal. It's called hepatic lipidosis, or fatty liver disease.

Hepatic lipidosis isn't just a problem with dieting cats, either. It's also a problem with sick cats who cannot or will not eat. And it can rear its fatty head when people switch cat foods and think, 'If the cat gets hungry enough, she'll eat.' A cat can and will starve herself into this potentially fatal condition.

To be safe, cats should lose weight gradually – no more than 1 percent of their body weight per week. (And we do mean gradually: That formula translates to a 15-pound cat losing just 2.4 ounces a week!) The goal is to drop the excess over a period of five or six months.

The best approach to weight loss in cats is a combination of moderate calorie restriction – ask your veterinarian for dietary guidance – and increased exercise. Yes, you can exercise a cat. Try throwing a mouse-shaped toy or playing with a fishing pole-type toy – anything to get puss up and moving.

IS THAT CAT FAT?

Is your cat fat? An ideal weight for most cats is eight to twelve pounds. Even the proverbial big-boned cat is likely obese if he weighs more than about fifteen pounds.

Of course, it does depend on the cat. That's why proper weight for cats is determined using a method called Body Conditioning Scoring (BCS).

Under the BCS system, a cat is at his normal weight if you can easily feel his ribs but they still have a slight cover of fat. A cat of healthy weight will also have a tuck-in behind the rib cage, making for a well-defined waist.

At the high end of the BCS scale, an obese cat has ribs that are difficult to feel under all the fat. From the top, his back could be used as a coffee table, and from the side view, fat is hanging down under his belly.

If you're not sure, have your cat checked out by the skilled hands and eyes (not to mention scales) of a veterinarian.

By the way, you can monitor your cat's weight loss at home by weighing yourself while holding the cat, and then putting kitty down and weighing yourself again — perhaps to your mutual benefit.

Q Everyone seems to be talking about fat cats and the problems obesity causes. But what about skinny cats?

A There are no stick-thin cat models on TV and cats don't have a bikini season. Can a cat be too skinny? Yes! A healthy cat should have a small – yes, small! – amount of fat padding over the ribs. When you press in just a little and move that skin back and forth over the ribs the way you'd move a shirt over the ridges of a washboard, you should be able to feel those ribs. A cat who's too skinny – and especially a cat who loses weight quickly – needs to see the veterinarian.

When an older cat becomes skinny, it may be a relatively common malady called hyperthyroidism. In cats with this disease, the thyroid gland starts overproducing its special hormone, making these cats lose weight and often seem to be more active than normal for an older cat. Veterinarians sometimes call the condition 'zoom around the room' syndrome. Left untreated, hyperthyroidism can be deadly. Fortunately, treating the disease is a real veterinary success story.

The overactive thyroid can be persuaded to slow down using drugs, surgery or radiation therapy. Radiation therapy involves a hospital stay, but usually resolves the problem permanently. Other pet lovers decide on surgery or daily medication. If you're facing this decision, discuss all the options with your veterinarian and choose what's right for you and your cat.

Hyperthyroidism is what makes many cats look like a rack of bones, but it's certainly not the only possible problem. The cat could have a digestive problem, suffer from a severe internal parasite infestation, even have an autoimmune problem such as FIV (a feline form of AIDS). If you're free-feeding in a multicat household, your skinny cat may simply be losing out at the trough!

Bottom line: A cat who's too fat or too skinny needs to be checked out by a veterinarian.

Q Why do cats insist that bedtime is playtime?

A Because a cat is a creature of the night . . . or at least, the twilight. Cats sleep all day – and most of the night – just so they can be at their liveliest when the sun is setting. The early bird may get the worm, but it's the late-night kitty who scores the mouse.

While many cats eventually figure out that we're not much fun after dark, some never do stop pestering their owners to play. Especially young cats, who just don't understand why you're so willing to cash in your chips when the night is still young. Cats are preprogrammed to hunt when the sun goes down. And since hunting and play are the same thing to them, their little brains are thinking, 'Party, party, PARTY!'

Want to sleep? Try playing with your cat an hour or so before bedtime to take the edge off the kitty crazies. (Not only before bedtime, though, or your cat will be bouncing off the walls just as you're trying to sleep. Cats need two or three play sessions a day.)

You can also feed your cat his biggest meal of wet food immediately before your bedtime, to give you a head start and to take advantage of the natural tendency of cats (and people) to feel a little sleepy after a meal.

Q Do all cats groom themselves or are some cats slobs?

A Cats like to keep their coat in good shape. In fact, when a cat starts losing interest in grooming, it can be a sign there's something wrong with her, physically. In particular, fat cats have a propensity to become slovenly or they're so huge, like a fur-covered balloon of sorts, they simply can't reach around the curve of their ample bodies to groom. If your cat looks tired and tattered, take her to the vet.

One of the more interesting things about cats is that most will groom themselves in a particular order. Grooming starts when a cat licks her lips and then wets the side of her paw. She will then run the damp paw over the side of her face and behind her ear (like a washcloth), and then repeat the same sequence on the opposite side.

Next, she'll lick her front legs, shoulders and flanks. Then it's one leg up and then the other, to get to all those personal spots. The whole thing wraps up with a trip down to the end of the tail.

Kittens get a free ride on grooming until they're about six weeks of age; their moms do all the hard work for them. In fact, for the first few days she even licks their anus. (That should be enough to get her on the TV show *The Worst Jobs in History.*) Her job is about more than motherly love and good housekeeping: When kittens are newborns, their mom's tongue is what stimulates them to eliminate.

While all cats try to keep up their appearance, good grooming can be more difficult for older cats, obese cats and cats with long, silky coats. These cats need help from their owners to maintain that just-licked look. The good news is that grooming your cat can be a pleasurable bonding experience for you both.

Cats lick themselves clean right after dinner because instinct has taught them the sooner they remove food odors, the less likely that predators will get a whiff of McCat.

Q Do cats ever really need a bath?

A A lot of cats go their whole lives without ever being dunked intentionally in water. Still, there are a few good reasons why you might consider giving your cat a bath, plus a few reasons that are not so good: You feel like giving blood; you want to see what the cat looks like on the ceiling; or you want one of those angry cat photos to put on the Internet.

Back to the good reasons. If someone in your family is allergic to cats, weekly bathing with plain water will help make life easier – for the person, not the cat. Your cat will also need a bath if he gets into something he can't clean off himself, either because it's too sticky or because it's not safe. If your cat has a skin condition or external parasites, he may require a medicated bath.

And then there are those breeds of cats we've 'improved' through selective breeding. Some of these silky, longhaired beauties (Persians come to mind) just can't keep up with grooming on their own. In addition to regular combing and brushing, they may need an occasional bath.

Can you bathe a cat and still end up in one piece? Truth to tell, it's a lot easier if you get the cat used to all kinds of handling – from bathing and brushing to combing and nail trims –

from kittenhood on. That's what people who show cats do. If you're faced with a cat who has to be bathed and will fight you tooth and nail, do what any sensible person does: Call a groomer.

Alternately, make it a two-person job. Wear long sleeves, draw a warm water bath in the kitchen sink, and set out the shampoo and towels before you get your cat. The cat-holder should grab the pet by the nape of the neck firmly and decisively and . . . oh! did we mention bandages? Set out some bandages, too. You're going to need them.

But seriously . . . keep your hold firm on the nape – you'll be holding your cat where a mom cat holds a kitten – and ease your cat into the water. Soap quickly, rinse well. Towel if you can, but if not, just let go and watch the cat take off like an Olympic sprinter for the farthest, darkest corner of the house.

GETTING OUT WHAT YOUR CAT GETS INTO

Sometimes you have to give a cat a real bath, no getting around it. But other times you can safely remove stubborn debris from your cat with some common household products.

For example, if your cat has a mat (a little tangle of fur that looks like the beginning of a dreadlock, mon), work some cornstarch into the mess, slice through the mat a couple of times from the skin out with scissors and then gently pick it apart. (If your cat is one big mat, it's likely kinder to have a groomer shave him into a lion cut — short on the body with a little mane — and start fresh, rather than try to remove all the mats.)

If your cat has gotten into chewing gum, try peanut butter to lubricate the mess and ease the gum from the fur. Anything petroleum-based is probably better dealt with by your veterinarian, since cats are very sensitive to these products.

Last, but not least, rolling in feces. This is generally a bigger problem for dogs than for cats, since cats show more sense in leaving muck alone.

The best treatment for this problem is to take 1 quart of 3-percent hydrogen peroxide (available from any drugstore), 1/4 cup of baking soda (sodium bicarbonate, for you science types), and 1 teaspoon of liquid soap, such as Dove. Mix and immediately apply, while still fizzing, to the stinky pet. Rinse thoroughly with tap water.

What about that old standby, tomato juice? You'll end up with a pink cat who still stinks — just not quite as much.

Q Why do cats hate to be in water?

A Domestic cats are descended from desert dwellers, and they see no reason why anyone should waste any energy swimming. They're perfectly capable of swimming, and in fact cats are good swimmers. But they seem to know that it not only makes them look silly, but also requires at least an hour of careful and determined grooming to get every hair back in place and restore a cat's dignity and scent to normal levels.

Sure, tigers swim, and some even seem to like it. Of course, there's nothing you can do to a tiger that would make the animal look less than majestic. But a domestic cat? Few things look sillier than a soaking-wet, seething cat pretending to be dignified.

Oddly enough, one breed of cat apparently didn't get the memo that all cats should hate water. Turkish Vans (a breed that developed around Lake Van – hint, hint) like to swim, and in their native land they are known as 'the swimming cats' because of this highly unusual trait.

Q Why are some cats so chatty?

A Probably because they're Siamese! Truly, this is one of those funny things that makes the world go around. One reason why people who wouldn't have any cat except a Siamese feel that way is because they love having a pet who is so talkative. To other cat lovers, that famous Siamese chattiness would drive them crazy.

Siamese are probably best known of the feline chatty Cathies, but that's also because they're the most popular of the Oriental family of cat breeds. Others in this general group share with the Siamese not only their gift of the gab, but also their long, slender bodies and agile, active personalities.

If you like a cat who'll keep up her end of the conversation, you should consider not only a Siamese but also a Balinese, Oriental and colorpoint shorthairs, Bombay, Burmese, and the three varieties of rex cats. Abyssinians and their longhaired cousins, Somalis, can also be talkative.

If you want a quiet cat, find one with a heavier build (naturally heavy, we mean – not a fat cat). These cats, which include such breeds as the Persian, Maine coon cat, and Norwegian forest cat, tend to be quieter and less active then their smaller, slinkier sisters.

Of course, if you're not careful, you can take a relatively quiet cat and accidentally train her to be noisy. This typically happens when you reward her meowing with a big payoff – food, perhaps, or playtime, or an opened door. Don't say we didn't warn you!

Q   What's the most common coat pattern in cats?

A   Humans have long had a desire to meddle with other animals, and that's certainly true of the cat. While we've been content overall to leave most cats in a pretty predictable size and shape – especially when you consider what we've done with dogs – we've certainly done a lot with the feline coat. Consider this: The Cat Fanciers' Association lists more than sixty color patterns for the Persian alone.

However, paws down, the tabby rules. Those tiger-striped markings are the original pattern of our cats' ancestors, and they can still be observed on some wild relatives of the domestic cat.

Tabbies come in several distinct patterns and many colors, including red (more commonly called orange, ginger or marmalade), cream, brown and gray. The tabby pattern is so dominant that, even in solid-colored cats, if you squint a little you can often discern faint tabby markings, especially on the head, legs and tail.

The word 'tabby' comes from Atabi, a silk imported to Britain long ago that had a striped pattern similar to that of the domestic cat.

Q Are all tortoiseshell cats female?

A Almost all tortoiseshell and tortoiseshell-on-white cats are female, but not quite all. About 1 in every 3,000 calico cats is a male . . . sort of.

Before we go any further, though, let's make sure we all agree on what we're talking about. A tortoiseshell cat has patches of orange or red and patches of black, chocolate or cinnamon. Throw in a white background color – that is, a basically white cat with tortoiseshell patches – and you have a tortoiseshell-on-white cat. In the US, tortoiseshell-on-white is called calico. Tortoiseshell and calico are not specific breeds of cat; they're color patterns.

Now that we're all clear, let's consider the genetics of cat coat color – a very complex subject indeed. The gene that governs how a cat's red/orange color is displayed is on the X chromosome. A female cat has two X chromosomes and a male cat has one X and one Y. Thus, any cat, male or female, can be orange.

In males, however, that color is usually expressed in one way: the tabby pattern, often called a ginger tom or marmalade tabby. It takes two X chromosomes to make a calico or a tortoiseshell, which is why the overwhelming majority of calico cats are female.

Every now and then, though, you get a male cat who has not

only X and Y chromosomes like a normal guy, but also an extra X chromosome. This unusual genetic arrangement is called Klinefelter's syndrome, and it happens in other species as well. If a Klinefelter male cat has orange/ red coding on both his X chromosomes, he'll be a calico or tortoiseshell cat.

In female cats, the red/orange color can be expressed in any of three ways: an orange tabby, a tortoiseshell, or a calico. People sometimes think that almost all orange tabbies are male, just as almost all calicos are female. Not true. It's a lot more common for an orange tabby to be female than it is for a calico to be male.

CALICO, HE WASN'T

When I was a young girl, I wanted a calico cat. I cut out pictures of calicos and glued them onto construction paper; these I put all over my bedroom walls. I took out every library book I could find that featured a calico cat, and needed but three colors to fill in the lines on my cat coloring book: white, orange and black.

When my parents finally said I could have a cat, I was as happy as a little girl could be. I made a special bed for my new kitten-to-be and took out even more books from the library on how to care for her properly — yes, her, because I knew from reading that my calico would be a girl.

Dad had a coworker who was giving away kittens, and not long after, he brought one of them home. Gray and black tiger stripe, white bib, and white paws. They had missed (or ignored?) every clue I thought was beyond obvious. I fussed for a bit, but figured maybe I'd better quit while I was ahead, especially since my parents suggested that if I didn't like this kitten, maybe I didn't need a kitten at all.

I named him Calico, and we grew up together, good friends until the end. I still have a fondness for calicos and tortoiseshells, but I know better than to judge a cat by his color.

— Gina Spadafori

Q *Are all white cats deaf?*

A Not all white cats are deaf, but it's certainly not uncommon. White cats with blue eyes are more likely to be deaf than white cats with eyes of any other color.

Deaf animals can make fine pets, but they need to be protected from hazards they can't hear. For a deaf cat, that means an indoor life is the only safe choice. Although they can't hear the sound of the can opener or the treats shaking in their box, deaf cats can adapt amazingly well. They can even feel the vibrations as you make your way to the kitchen treat drawer.

The link between white (and blue-gray) fur and deafness is also common in dogs, by the way, especially when the white patch is over the ear.

Q *Who invented kitty litter?*

A Edward Lowe. And because of him, millions of cats are able to live indoors, safe and sound, in sunny windowsills and on comfy chairs, where they know they belong.

While some sources say Lowe wasn't the first person to come up with the idea of keeping a box in the house where a cat could eliminate – some people used garden dirt or sand, and at least one other inventor tried shredded paper – Lowe was the one who hit the jackpot.

Lowe worked for his father's company, which sold industrial absorbents, including products such as sawdust and an absorbent clay called Fuller's Earth. One day his neighbor asked him if he could suggest something clean for her cat's box. She had been using ash, and the cat was tracking ashy footprints all over the house. Lowe suggested Fuller's Earth, and it worked like a charm.

Lowe decided he was on to something. So in 1947 he put the clay in five-pound bags, wrote 'Kitty Litter' on the front, and suggested to a local store owner that he sell the bags of clay for 65 cents – at a time when sand went for a penny a pound. The owner laughed, so Lowe changed strategies: 'Give it away,' he said, 'and see how it does.'

It was a smart bet. Lowe died a millionaire many times over, after selling his company to a multinational conglomerate. Today, sales of cat-box fillers top $700 million a year – and Lowe's Kitty Litter still takes home a fair chunk of that money.

According to a survey by the American Pet Products Manufacturers Association, 83 percent of cat owners have litter boxes for their pets. The kind of box filler Lowe pioneered is no longer the most popular, though: Clumping litter makes up nearly three-quarters of the market these days.

Q Who hears better — cats, dogs or humans?

A The winner is . . . cats. Cats can hear nearly three times more frequencies than humans can. For you technical types, cats' hearing stops at 80 kilohertz, dogs' at 45 kHz, and humans' at a pathetic 20 kHz. Because cats can rotate their ears and focus each ear independently, they also can hear well from all directions.

Well, sure, but we can wear earrings. On the other hand, cats in ancient Egypt also wore earrings.

A cat's hearing is so sensitive that some pets will leave the room when a TV or radio is on too loudly for their comfort. And don't even think of starting the vacuum!

If you figure this means your cat can hear you perfectly well when you call her, you're absolutely right. Like a teenager or your partner who's engrossed in the TV, she's just ignoring you.

Kittens are born blind and deaf. They don't begin hearing until about two weeks of age. Once a kitten can hear, though, she can hear things we can only imagine: bats in flight or a mouse in the brush up to 30 feet away.

Q Where did the nine lives myth come from?

A Cats have proven to be an incredibly successful species. From their origins as desert dwellers, they can now be found nearly everywhere, in just about every climate. Perhaps this is why we first got the idea that cats have more than one chance at life.

Look at it another way and it's clear that the cat's formidable survival skills enabled many of them to escape what looked like certain death. With their finely tuned senses, cats can spot the first hint of trouble and get lost before things get really bad. They can skedaddle with a blinding burst of speed for short distances, and they can go up a tree or over a fence before whatever's after them has time to react. With their slender, lithe bodies, they can wriggle through holes the size of their heads, getting themselves out of trouble almost as quickly as they seem to get into it. They're finicky eaters, which sometimes protects them from poisoning. And if they fall, they can usually right themselves in midair to stick a four-point landing.

Cats generally and wisely believe that discretion is the better part of valor. A cat in trouble would, sensibly, rather run than fight. But corner a cat and look out: With sharp teeth and claws, these animals can put up quite a fight.

Every cat comes equipped with an amazing arsenal of

survival skills and an instinctive ability to look out for himself. But even with all these advantages, every cat, like you and me, has but one life to live.

More than 300,000 cat mummies were found in one Egyptian temple in 1850, and tons of cat mummies were shipped to Britain to be used as fertilizer. We suppose that made the plants leap out of the ground.

Q *Dogs have that neat 'seven years equals one human year' formula. How do you measure a cat's age?*

A There isn't an easy formula for cats – and even that old 'dog years' thing doesn't work as well as most people think it does.

Some people use a 'one year equals four' formula, figuring that a twenty-year-old cat is about equivalent to an eighty-year-old person. The problem is that a one-year-old cat is actually the equivalent, in terms of mental and physical maturity, of a human fifteen-year-old. But 'fifteen cat years equals one human year' would mean a ten-year-old cat is like a 150-year-old person. Clearly, that formula is not going to work!

A better equation is to count the first year of a cat's life as being comparable to the time a human reaches the early stages of adulthood. Like a human adolescent, a year-old cat looks fairly grown up and is physically capable of becoming a parent, but lacks emotional maturity.

The second year of a cat's life takes puss to the first stages of full adulthood in humans – a two-year-old cat is roughly equivalent to a person in their mid-twenties.

From there, the 'four equals one' rule works pretty well. A

cat age three is still young – comparable to a person of twenty-nine. A six-year-old cat, similar to a forty-one-year-old person, is in the throes of middle age; a twelve-year-old cat, similar to a sixty-five-year-old person, has earned the right to slow down a little.

It's all relative, though. Some cats live more risky lives than others. Feral cats – those poor, flea-bitten creatures wandering anywhere food can be scrounged, are lucky to live more than a year or two before being claimed by accident, predation or disease. Pet cats who are allowed to roam are also more likely to meet with an early demise. With regular veterinary care and good nutrition, protected indoor cats can easily live into their late teens.

Q Are dogs and cats really mortal enemies, or is that just the stuff of Saturday morning cartoons?

A Cats occupy a fairly interesting ecological niche, right in the middle of the food chain: They are both predators and prey. Their skills as a predator are obvious, but to many bigger predators – especially urban foxes and some dogs – a cat pretty much looks like a tricky-to-catch but still tasty lunch. Some dogs are more into the prey thing than others, but for dogs who like to hunt for themselves, a cat is just another item on the menu. As the saying goes, 'It's strictly business, nothing personal.'

Some cats have been known to attack dogs, too, although generally it's preemptive self-defense – or a very small dog indeed.

Aside from dogs who consider cats to be prey, there are dogs who will naturally chase anything that moves, from a squirrel to a bicyclist to a plastic bag blowing in the wind. These dogs will happily chase a cat and may even bite if they catch one, but would probably back up and back off if faced with a cat in full defensive mode: back arched, teeth bared, every hair standing on end and those razor-sharp claws unsheathed.

Cats who are raised around dogs are generally fine with them, and in many homes cats and dogs become friends and even snuggle buddies. A cat who hasn't had to put up with a dog probably won't welcome having one join the family, but with slow and careful introductions, the cat will probably adjust.

Many animal shelters and rescue groups have a 'test cat,' the feline equivalent of the lovable Labrador retriever, who is relaxed enough to accept the short-term annoyance of being introduced to dogs, in the interest of gauging the canine's level of interest in cats.

Q Are these programs for trapping and releasing feral cats really such a good idea? Wouldn't it be kinder to put the cats to sleep?

A Every community has what are called feral cats – abandoned pets and their offspring. Although many people figure cats can take care of themselves and dump their pets when they no longer want them, the fact is that the lives of feral cats are full of danger and fear – and often those nine lives tick off faster than the sweep hand of a stopwatch.

There have always been kind-hearted people who feed homeless cats, even if it's just sharing a tuna sandwich from a park bench. There have also always been people who find colonies of feral cats to be annoying; they make noise, they spray urine, they multiply like . . . well . . . cats.

There was a time when municipalities handled feral cat colonies by putting out poison or trapping all the cats and dropping them off at the local shelter – whether they were adoptable or not. More recently, though, the trend has been toward a more humane way to handle feral cats called TNR, which stands for 'trap, neuter and return.'

TNR advocates argue that just feeding feral cats makes the problem worse, but that trapping and killing the cats doesn't work in the long run to solve the problem.

Instead, they trap the cats, place the ones they can in caring homes, and return the rest after they've been neutered and immunized. These colonies can then be fed and cared for in a hands-off but humane way, and their numbers dwindle naturally because the reproductive taps have been turned off for good.

Trap, neuter and return programs for feral cats seems counterintuitive to many people. If you don't want cats around, wouldn't it make sense just to remove them permanently? As it turns out . . . no.

When you remove cats, other animals take their place. That's because the food source that attracted the cats will still be there, which means more cats (or rats or foxes) will eventually show up. Meanwhile, studies have shown that trapping feral cats, finding homes for the ones you can and neutering the rest before returning them to their colonies really does reduce their numbers.

Neutering reduces the fighting, yowling and spraying behaviors, many of which are associated with fighting over mates. The neutered cats defend their territory, too, and prevent other animals from moving in – including unneutered cats. Think of them as flashing furry gang colors, ready to make war but unable to make love. (The colony caretakers are quick to remove and find homes for any abandoned pets who turn up, as well as any kittens.)

While such programs aren't perfect, they have been shown to be both more humane and more effective than past efforts to simply exterminate feral cats. Alley Cat Allies is perhaps the most influential group when it comes to advocating for and training community groups how to run such programs. There's plenty of information on their Web site (www.alleycat.org), including studies of TNR programs and how well they've done.

Q Can kittens born in the wild really be tamed to be good pets?

A Absolutely! Adults born wild usually cannot adjust to life as a pet. But the kittens . . . these are the success stories.

If trapped young and handled lovingly, these little ones can make the transition back into human society and become pets every bit as loving as a cat born in someone's home. So if you have an eye on a little purrster at an adoption fair but wonder about his feral beginnings . . . we say: Go for him! It's likely to be the start of a purrfect friendship.

By the way, adult cats newly dumped can often be trapped and placed in homes, as well. These poor guys are usually terrified and bewildered about being outside, and want nothing more than to be back indoors as somebody's pet.

Q If a cat's temperature is higher than ours, why does my cat spend so much time lying in the sun?

A Because cats are the ultimate sun worshippers. They're descended from desert animals, and their wild ancestors liked to bask all day and hunt when the sun went down. For our cats, the call of the wild sometimes means feeling the sun on their lovely, glossy fur as their irises close to mere slits – like feline stoners – to protect their eyes.

This attraction can sometimes get them into trouble, though. Cats have died because of their desire to find a warm, cozy spot. They've snuggled up to warm car engines on cold nights or snuck into clothes dryers to bury themselves in a warm pile of clothes – and been killed when the car or the dryer is restarted without anyone realizing the cat is inside.

Sadly, these kinds of accidents are not uncommon. They're easy to prevent, though. Keep the dryer door closed and check inside before you put anything into it and again before you turn it on. Before you start the car, thump the car hood and honk the horn to scatter whatever cat may be sleeping within.

The average body temperature of a cat is about 102 degrees Fahrenheit, and her heart beats about 155 times per minute.

Q Can curiosity really kill a cat? Just how curious are cats?

A Curiosity has definitely done in more than a few cats. Although cats do have keen survival skills and are picky enough to avoid many poisons (antifreeze being a notable exception, because it just doesn't smell bad or taste yucky enough to put cats off), they sometimes get themselves into trouble because they're investigating something that might be worth chasing, especially anything that darts, scurries or flutters. That's what predators do, after all – they detect, pursue, attack and kill prey.

And in so doing, they can run into the path of an oncoming car or a waiting dog, fall from a great height, end up trapped in a wall or a basement, meet a strange cat with an infectious disease to which they don't have adequate immunity, or even find themselves looking at a wild animal (or a neighbor) who doesn't like cats at all. In such cases, curiosity can indeed kill a cat.

Antifreeze is an equal-opportunity killer; not only are cats its victims, but also other pets, wildlife and even children, because the liquid is a bright color and is quite sweet. Once even a small amount is licked, the toxic effects are difficult to reverse.

Some states have mandated that antifreeze manufacturers add a 'bittering' agent that makes the stuff unpalatable. Seems like a great idea to us. In the meantime, you might consider using a safer antifreeze made from propylene glycol or simply keeping your cat indoors.

Q Why do a cat's whiskers twitch?

A A cat's whiskers are deep-set, hypersensitive modified hairs called vibrissae (great Scrabble word) that help kitty find her way in the world. How sensitive? A cat's whiskers can detect small changes in air currents. They are an important sense organ, so keep cats away from open flames that may light the whiskers up like a sparkler and keep your junior barber-to-be away from the cat.

The spread of a cat's whiskers helps her gauge how much room she needs to fit through a narrow opening at a trot in very low light. Of course, this isn't fool-proof: When a cat gains weight, her whiskers don't get longer so her head may clear but her body may get stuck.

Your cat's whiskers can also help clue you in on what she's thinking. When the whiskers are forward, a cat is in a friendly or curious mood. When the whiskers are pinned back, look out!

When your cat's whiskers are moving during a nap, you can tell she has entered the deepest kind of sleep, which is accompanied by rapid eye movements – and probably, dreams.

Q How can I make my cat like me more? He ignores me most of the time, except when he wants to be fed.

A You've heard the trite saying: Dogs come when they're called, cats say, 'Leave a message, I'll get back to you.' That's not true of all cats. But cats, like people, have different personalities. Some are more outgoing than others.

Unlike dogs (and some people), many cats are not 'automatically' friendly. Instead, they are automatically wary. And some cats enjoy your company, but on their terms. They may not love snuggling or being picked up, but if you let them express their affection in their own way, you may find that they always follow you from room to room or like to sit on the same piece of furniture you're sitting on. You need to recognize and appreciate the signs of feline love.

To a certain extent, you're only going to have so much luck when it comes to making your cat show his affection on your terms. There are a few tricks you can use, though.

Make sure your interactions aren't threatening to your cat. Don't look him directly in the eye and don't force yourself on or grab at your cat. When you talk to your cat, use a soft, soothing voice.

Focus your attention on petting that your cat finds pleasurable – behind the ears, along the chin, down the back. Avoid tummy rubs, which most cats don't like, or you'll find the cat drawing hieroglyphics on your arms and hands with his claws. Keep these petting sessions short and build on your successes. Watch your cat's tail tip: When it starts to twitch, let him leave.

Play with your cat. Interactive games using a fishing pole-type toy (a bit of feather or fluff on a string) can be very entertaining for you both. Again, let your cat determine the length of the play session.

Groom your cat. Gentle brushing feels nice to a cat – and keeps the shedding and hairballs down, too. At first, stick to the areas a cat most enjoys having touched: Under the chin, along the sides of the face and the flanks are usually safe. Be slow, gentle and rhythmic with your motions. Talk softly to your cat while you're brushing him.

Good relationships take time to develop, and with a cat, they must all be on his terms. Most cats can learn to recognize their owners as a source of good things, and that means they'll start to turn on the charm when they see you. Be sure to give your cat attention when he asks for it; that way, he's certain to ask again.

And don't forget the value of the occasional treat. Chocolate is the famed elixir of love for humans. Could bits of savory salmon or steak do the trick for puss?

Q *Why do ragdoll cats go limp when you hold them? How do they do that?*

A A lot of – how can we say it kindly? – porkies get passed around about cat breeds (dog breeds too), and some of them seem to take on a life of their own. We've read claims that rex cats are hypoallergenic (sorry, no), and that ragdolls go limp when they're picked up because of some genetic mutation in their nervous system. An alternate theory that can be found in the strange, dark corners of the Internet is that the cats were mated with aliens or had human genes spliced in. Um . . . no.

Ragdoll cats are prized for their laid-back personality, and the mellowest of these beauties have been used in breeding programs over the years, making an easygoing cat even more so. But there's no mutation behind that ragdoll flop and not all ragdolls are floppers.

The ones that are, however, are a major armful of fluffy feline love – they just relax into your arms when you pick them up.

RACCOON LOVE CHILD?

There's an old story that the Maine coon cat is the result of long-ago matings between cats and raccoons. Old wives' tale?

You bet! The Maine coon cat is an American original — just not quite that original. This hardy, longhaired breed developed as an all-purpose, all-weather New England farm cat and companion. The markings for which the breed is best known — a distinctive tabby — does leave the cat with a fluffy tail that somewhat resembles the tail of a raccoon. But that's as far as it goes. The Maine coon is all cat. (Another improbable theory holds that the cat was the result of crossbreedings between ship cats and North American bobcats. Also not true.)

Although in recent years more exotic pedigreed cats, such as the Persian, have eclipsed the hardy Yankee cat, the winner of the very first cat show held in the United States was a Maine coon by the name of Cosey.

Maine coons come in all sorts of colors and patterns besides their raccoon impersonations, by the way. The cats are one of the largest breeds and are known for their easygoing disposition.

Q *My cat jumps from the floor right to the top of my bookshelf. How is that possible?*

A Many cats love to be high – and we're not talking about catnip. And getting high's no problem when you can jump several times your own height and land gracefully and accurately on a piece of real estate not much bigger than a half-sheet of paper.

Cats are incredibly athletic. That big jump comes from their powerful thigh muscles, which constrict tightly and then let go like a catapult. Watch a cat, they coil. A human with the leg strength and power of a cat could jump from the ground to the top of a house – the only problem is that his thighs would be as big as his waist.

You saw *Lion King*, didn't you, with lofty Pride Rock? The jumping power enables cats to put themselves up above it all, where they feel secure and can see everything that's going on. On top of the bookshelf is a safe place to be when the dog or the kids are on the rampage or the vacuum cleaner is roaring – just like on top of the garden wall is a great place to be when you're watching for little mousies in the grass. We're guessing being up high also meshes well with a cat's natural superior attitude. They like to look down on us.

The desire to go higher is stronger in some cats than in others. Among pedigreed cats, the slender, athletic cats of the Oriental varieties, such as Abyssinians and Siamese, are born to jump. Cats with larger, heavier bodies – such as Persians – are more likely to consider a jump onto the couch to be high enough. And fat cats, well, in their dreams they leap, but in reality they sleep.

Like kids at their first dance recital, not all cats are as graceful as they think they are. If you live with a cat who's a bit clumsy, always bumping things off the shelves, you need to take action to prevent your favorite knick-knacks from being knocked down. Your most delicate, darling and irreplaceable items are best kept behind doors in glass-fronted cabinets. For the others, get a product called Blu tack. It will keep your cat out of the doghouse.

Q When I'm petting my cat, she sometimes goes from relaxed and purring to biting in an instant. What's up with that?

A As much as cats love to be petted, they can tolerate only so much. Many cats can quickly become over-stimulated by heavy petting and bite (or slap or swat) the hand that strokes them. Both genetics and social factors contribute to how likely a cat is to bite or swat while being petted. Some cats are born with short fuses; others are made that way (or made worse) through a lack of early socialization or proper training in kittenhood.

For some cats, the transition from 'come hither' to 'go thither' lasts about a nanosecond. Others give several clear warnings before they take matters into their own paws. But no matter how much of a hair trigger there is on your cat's attack mode, you can work to increase puss's tolerance for petting by paying close attention to her body language as you slowly increase the amount of time during which she'll calmly accept your attention.

For a highly reactive cat, don't pick her up for petting; just settle down next to her. Don't do anything else while you're petting her, either, such as watching TV. You want to pay attention to her body language so you can see exactly when she has reached her limit.

Restrict your caresses at first to less reactive areas of the body: behind the ears, under the chin and at the base of the tail (a spot that may cause the endearing lifting of the rear known as 'elevator butt'). A long stroke down the back is too much for some kitties, and you're really taking chances when you decide to tickle your cat's tummy.

Watch for signs that your cat has had enough: a tail flick, a twitch of the skin or ears, the whiskers rotating forward. When you get that early warning sign, show some respect and stop petting immediately. Let your cat leave if she wants to, or she'll enforce her preferences.

The idea is to gradually work up to longer petting sessions that always stop just short of the point where your pet becomes uncomfortable. For some cats, offering a tasty treat during petting can make a good thing even better.

If you miss the signs and end up in your cat's non-affectionate embrace, just freeze. Providing no resistance will help calm your cat and she'll just let go, usually in a few seconds. If you fight back or physically punish your cat, you are more likely to get bitten or scratched in the short run and damage your relationship with your pet in the long run.

Rolling over to show the belly is not an invitation to touch. In most cats, contact with the tummy triggers an instinctive reaction that involves teeth and claws.

Q Do cats purr only when they're happy?

A Expert cat observers know that purring isn't just a sound of contentment. Cats also purr when they're injured, while giving birth – even when they're dying. Purring has been described as something a cat does when he's with a friend or needs a friend, is happy or is in pain. It seems to be a sound that both conveys and creates comfort.

A couple more interesting facts about purring: While all the smaller cats, including servals and ocelots, purr, some of the big cats can't. Lions and tigers can roar and rumble, but they can't purr on the inhale and the exhale the way a little cat can. Little cats purr, but they can't roar. We think the little guys got the better part of the deal.

No one can completely explain the mechanics of a cat's purr. It remains a scientific mystery. Best guess: The sound is caused by the passing of air over structures in a cat's voice box.

A purring cat can lower a person's blood pressure, and relaxes both the cat and the person petting him. There is even some evidence that purring can help speed the healing process in cats.

Cats purr at a frequency of twenty-five vibrations per second.

Q Do cats really need to drink milk?

A We've all seen those charming Victorian images of farm kittens lapping up a saucer of milk, little milk-staches forming on their cute mouths. Yes, it's adorable. But back to reality, folks. Is cow's milk the perfect food for cats? Not at all!

On the contrary, some cats (like some people) can't tolerate milk products, and they'll have explosive diarrhea that can paint the walls of the farmhouse. For these animals, a saucer of milk means gastric upset.

In the wild, kittens never drink milk after they're weaned (and never drink cow's milk at all), and domestic cats have no reason to either. The inability to digest milk usually starts at about the age of twelve weeks.

On the other hand, if your cat likes and can tolerate milk, feel free to offer it as an occasional treat. Milk is a good source of protein and other nutrients for those cats who don't find it upsets their tummies. (Which means Garfield can enjoy his lasagne, cheese and all.) But if you never give milk to your cat, she's not missing anything important.

For kittens, though, mother's milk is the best there is – and cow's milk is no substitute. Besides essential nutrition, their mother's milk passes on life-protecting antibodies to the helpless newborns. (When weaning stops that source of immunity, your veterinarian will help boost your kitten's immune system with a series of kitten shots.)

Q What is it with crazy cat ladies? It seems like every day there's a news story about some person found with dozens of cats in her home.

A 'Crazy cat ladies' – and yes, most of these people are women – share a mental disorder known as hoarding, which is a form of obsessive-compulsive disorder. Although some people do get in over their heads when trying to rescue homeless animals of all species, hoarders typically end up with too many cats – perhaps because it's easy at first to hide a lot of cats in a home, perhaps because so many cats are homeless and are therefore easy to pick up, and perhaps because unneutered cats breed so prolifically.

As part of their illness, many hoarders don't recognize that their cats are living in overcrowded, horrible conditions. The neighbors do, because they're living next to a 2,500-square-foot litter box that isn't getting cleaned often enough or at all.

Some hoarders continue to take in more animals (sometimes representing themselves as a 'rescue' group) because they cannot bear the thought of any cat being put to death in a shelter. As their disease progresses, these people can completely lose

79

whatever grip they had on reality, to the point where they cannot even part with the bodies of their deceased cats.

By the time a hoarder is discovered by authorities, it's common to find unimaginable filth in the home; sick, dead and dying cats everywhere; and a person who is completely unable to recognize how awful things are.

If there's any silver lining in these tragic situations, it's that in recent years hoarding has been recognized as a mental illness, and humane enforcement and the courts are better able to handle such cases in a way that gets both the animals and the hoarder the help they need.

Not that it's a record any person should ever shoot for, but the highest number of cats found in a residence is 640, located in a home in Canada around 1993.

Q What is that 'Halloween cat' posture about? Do cats really do that?

A They do – but they save it for very special occasions. Most cats would rather run than fight, especially if they're faced with something like a big dog. (The exceptions to the rather-run-than-fight rule: mating and cat-to-cat territory skirmishes.) Sometimes, though, a cat can't hop a fence or run for the hills. Maybe he's cornered, or maybe he's startled.

A cornered cat has some pretty formidable weaponry. But again, why risk injury?

Consider the Halloween cat: back arched, body oriented sideways (so it looks a lot bigger), fur standing straight up, tail fluffed, mouth wide open with teeth gleaming, hissing with lots of sounds like a car tire that's been slashed. It's the feline equivalent of a poker bluff. The poker player wants you to think he has something he doesn't – three aces – so you'll fold. The cat wants you to think he's bigger and a whole lot more dangerous than he really is. Again, the aim is to make you fold.

And it works a lot of the time, especially with a vet who's about to administer a pill or take the cat's rectal temperature. When another animal sees that defensive posture, he'll stop to rethink his hand and often will toss in his metaphorical chips. Even if the adversary just stops to think, that will often give a cat enough of a head start to hightail it out of there. If the bluff doesn't work, a rake across the nose with those Samurai claws might do the trick.

By the way, if you ever see your cat in such a state, let him be. No matter how much your cat loves you, an animal in full fight-or-flight mode will bite or scratch. If you have to grab him – to get him out of a dangerous area, for example – throw a blanket over him. Otherwise, let him chill out completely before you try to touch him.

Q **What's the best way to give medicine to a cat?**

A Very carefully.

No matter how much you and your cat hate the idea, at some point in your pet's life, you're going to come home from the veterinary clinic with that brown liquid medication or something that looks like a horse pill, and you're going to have to give that medicine to your cat.

Is it easy? Not really (except for the vet, who's just showing off). Is it necessary? You bet! Seeing your veterinarian and then not following through on care instructions is worse than a waste of money: It may be dangerous, even fatal, for your pet. Put another way, the prescriptions your veterinarian prescribes need to go in the cat, not in the cabinet.

Most times you're dealing with a pill. You can try the Sneak Method, attempting to disguise a pill in a bit of something yummy in hopes that your cat doesn't notice the pill inside. (A product call Pill Pockets is ideal for this, since they're yummy little treats with a spot to stuff a pill.) Watch your cat carefully for the spit-out before considering the procedure a success – it may not be, and cats can hold a pill in their mouths for a long time. In fact, the Sneak Method works a lot better for dogs, who tend to bolt down their food, than for cats, who eat carefully, considering every mouthful. Sneaking a pill past your cat can be very difficult.

The No-Nonsense Method is harder, but once you've mastered it, you will know for sure where the pill went. Take a firm but gentle grip on your cat's head from above, pry open her jaw with the index finger of your other hand and press the pill far enough back on the tongue to trigger swallowing. (A quick, light blow on the nostrils can also trigger the swallow reflex once the pill is in.) Although veterinarians can make pilling a cat look like an easy, one-person job, you're likely to find the task easier at first if you have someone else hold your cat while you pill her.

Some people have good luck with plastic pill guns. You load a pill on the tip, press it to the back of your cat's tongue and release with a push on the plunger. Look for these in pet supply stores or catalogs, or in the ads in the back of pet magazines. Follow any pilling of a cat with a syringe or two of fresh water in your cat's mouth, since recent studies suggest that'll get the pill where it needs to be quickly – in the stomach.

For liquid medication, be sure your veterinarian sends you home with some large syringes (needles removed). These are marked on the side to make measuring easy, and they make it easier to get liquid medicine in the right place (an eyedropper can also work). Raise your cat's muzzle with a firm but gentle hold on the top of the head and lift her lip on one side. Ease the tip of the syringe to the back of the throat and then release the liquid in a slow, steady motion. Your cat will swallow naturally; be sure to give her time to do so as you're administering the medicine.

If you absolutely cannot deal with giving your cat pills or liquid medication, talk to your veterinarian about having the medications prepared by what's called a compounding pharmacy. They'll take the medicine and turn it into a paste or liquid in a flavor your cat will like, such as Atlantic Salmon or Mother's Milk. For cats who are on lifelong medication for chronic conditions, yummy meds from a compounding pharmacy can improve the quality of life for all – and end the daily hassle of forcing a cat to take her pill.

Why does a cat always choose to approach the one person in the room who hates cats?

Cats are not crazy about direct eye contact. They find it intimidating and possibly rude. So . . . a cat walks into a room full of people he doesn't know. He's a friendly cat, so he'd like to say hello. But . . . everyone's staring. What's wrong with these people?

One person isn't staring. It's the one person in the room who doesn't like cats – which is why she's not looking at the cat. Everyone else likes cats and wishes the cat would come over for a head scratch. Pet lovers live to meet new pets who love them back; it makes them seem like the cat whisperer to their family, friends and themselves. The person who doesn't like cats either hasn't cared enough to notice the cat or is intentionally looking away in hopes the cat hasn't noticed her.

The cat notices the one person in the room polite enough not to stare. And that's the person he heads for.

Either that, or choosing the only person in the room who doesn't like cats is a cat's idea of a really good joke. You decide.

Among the world's most famous cat haters were Genghis Khan, Alexander the Great, Julius Caesar, Napoleon and Hitler. This gives you a good idea of what kinds of people hate cats. Mohammed, Leonardo da Vinci, Abraham Lincoln, Florence Nightingale, Sir Winston Churchill and Albert Schweitzer are among the most famous cat lovers.

Q Can vaccines kill cats?

A In recent years, cat lovers have been horrified by reports of deadly tumors caused by something that's supposed to save the lives of their pets – routine vaccinations. Unfortunately, the cancer known as vaccine-associated feline sarcoma, or feline vaccine-site sarcoma, is more than a rumor, and it has claimed the lives of some cats.

No one is quite sure why some cats have ended up with cancer at the site where they received a feline leukemia or rabies vaccine, but the risk is very low – about 1 cat per 10,000 vaccinated. The Vaccine-Associated Feline Sarcoma Task Force is studying the problem, but so far we have no definitive answers about why some cats develop the disease and what can be done to prevent it.

For this reason, and because of general concerns about the frequency at which pets were being vaccinated, the old protocol of annual 'shots' for cats has been changed in the US. Instead, the American Association of Feline Practitioners and the Academy of Feline Medicine recommend that an individual vaccine regimen be developed for each cat, after the initial series of kitten shots has been completed. They advise veterinarians to tailor their preventive-care regimen based on the life stage (kitten vs. adult vs. senior) and lifestyle (indoor, outdoor, show cat) of each individual cat; an indoor-only cat may need to be vaccinated against fewer diseases than one who goes outside every day, for example.

For many vaccines, after the initial series of shots brings a kitten's immunity up to par, boosters are then recommended at three-year intervals. Veterinarians are also advised to use individual vaccines (no combination shots, in other words) and to give the shots in different parts of the body to make it easier to identify and treat any possible reactions.

Talk to your veterinarian about what's right for your cat – exactly which vaccines are needed and how often your cat needs them. And remember that even if your cat no longer needs annual boosters, he still needs regular examinations (twice a year is recommended), which are an essential part of a preventive-care program.

It should be noted that most veterinarians (who are also pet lovers extraordinaire) continue to vaccinate their own cats. Why? Because vaccines protect against diseases that can kill cats. These veterinarians believe the risk from under-vaccinating is still far greater than that of over-vaccinating.

Q ## Is it true paracetamol can kill a cat?

A Yes, and so can aspirin and ibuprofen. Acetaminophen, the active ingredient in paracetamol, should never be given to a cat, nor should any over-the-counter human pain-control medicine. Many a well-meaning cat lover has tried to ease the pain of an older cat, only to lose them to a product that is a deadly poison to felines.

Two primary problems: First, cats don't metabolize these kinds of painkillers very well. And second, while one tablet might be the correct dose for a 150-pound human, the dose for a 10-pound cat is almost microscopically small. Even painkillers for infants are made for a child who weighs a lot more than a cat.

We understand the desire to care for your cat and save money, but it's essential to realize that cats and other pets are not people, and medications for people may not work in the same way. For these reasons, don't give any over-the-counter product or home remedy to a sick pet – at least not before first checking with your veterinarian.

Q When one of my cats comes home from the veterinarian, my other cat acts as if he's a complete stranger, hissing and spitting. Why?

A You know you have the right cat in that carrier, no switcheroos at the veterinary hospital. You've even checked the ID tags and felt the kink in his tail. But to the cat at home, the cat you brought in doesn't smell right. In fact, he smells worse than not right: He smells like a veterinary office, and you know what that smells like – competitor cats, dirty dogs, and an olfactory cocktail of horrible medicines and disinfectants. If that's not worth throwing a hissy fit over, we don't know what is.

Let the cat who's just home from the doctor settle down in a room by himself for an hour or two. Then you can try a couple of old cat rescuers' tricks to confuse both cats and bring peace to spitting parties.

One trick is to take a clean towel, rub it over one cat and then the other, and back again a couple of times. This will distribute the scents, both new and old, over both cats, and probably spark a round of grooming that will have them both so occupied that they'll forget what they're upset about. The other trick is to dab a drop of vanilla just below the noses of both cats. Again, it's a confuse-a-cat trick that often works.

In extreme cases, you may have to do an entire, full-scale reintroduction, isolating the cat who went to the veterinarian for a few days until both cats relax and accept each other again.

The collective term for a group of adult cats is called a clowder. Stick a mollusk in a get-together of cats and you'll have ... ahem ... clam clowder.

Q Every cute little kitten illustration seems to show a ball of yarn as a plaything. But I read recently that strings of all sorts are dangerous for cats. Is that true?

A The problem with string, yarn, ribbon and thread is that sometimes cats – especially playful young cats and kittens – swallow a section. And when that happens, your cat may end up in emergency surgery to have these playthings removed. Because when a piece of string becomes a wad of string, it has a difficult time traversing the gastrointestinal tract from point A (the mouth) to point B (let's call it 'down south'). In fact, it's very common for the intestines to bunch up around the string like a folded accordion, and this requires major surgery to remove the string and repair the damage.

If your cat loves to chase string, indulge her! But do so only when you are there to supervise. Fishing pole toys are wonderful for these games. A piece of ribbon or yarn is okay too. You just need to remember to put all these potentially dangerous playthings away in a secure spot when you're not there to play with your cat.

Be sure to put away all the gift-wrap ribbon and any craft projects involving needlework and knitting when you're not working on them, as well. And tinsel on the Christmas tree . . . forget about it.

One final caution: Use a covered trash container. Your cat may find the string from a pot roast irresistible. (You don't?)

Q *How can I get my cat to leave the houseplants alone? He pees in the pots and chews on the leaves.*

A Plants on the ground or on low tables are the easiest targets, so make your houseplants less accessible to a bored and wandering cat. Put plants up high, or better yet, hang them.

For the plants you can't move out of harm's way, make them less appealing by coating them with something your cat finds disagreeable. Cat-discouragers include Bitter Apple, a nasty-tasting substance available at any pet supply stores, and Tabasco sauce or vinegar from any grocery store. As soon as you find a taste your cat doesn't like, keep reapplying it to reinforce the point.

You can also discourage your pet by shooting him with the spray from a water bottle when you see him in the plants. (This works even better if you're able to hide and shoot, because the cat thinks there's some invisible guardian of the plants who lives in the house and can see him chewing them even when you're not around.) Be sure to squirt him only on the body and only with clean water.

Pot your plants in heavy, wide-bottomed containers, and cover the soil of the problem plants with rough decorative rock. That will keep your cat from using the dirt for a litter box.

CATS WHO LIKE VEGGIES

Noshing on greenery is a popular pastime for cats, and it's perfectly normal. Some have theorized that in nature cats and other carnivores ingest plant material from the bellies of prey animals. (Yet another thing cats like to eat that we probably prefer to pass on.) Other people think plants just taste good to cats, or that they like the feeling of grass and leaves in their mouths — kind of like kitty chewing gum.

If your cat goes outdoors, he's choosing his own greens to munch. Indoor cats will go for the houseplants if you don't provide them with greens of their own.

Wheat grass, the same stuff that's juiced up for health food smoothies, also goes by the name of cat grass. Lots of pet supply stores sell cat grass kits with seeds preplanted in a container. You just add water and set the planter on the windowsill. Many farmers' markets also sell small pots of cat grass.

Often, cats vomit up the greens soon after they eat them. It's all part of the pleasure — for a cat.

Q Can cats walk on a leash like dogs?

A Not exactly. With patience, praise and treats, many cats can learn to tolerate a short walk on leash. Don't even try it with a collar, though: Use a figure-8 harness designed for cats. And know that, unlike dogs, who can generally be persuaded to go where you want to, when you're walking a cat it's really more like the cat is walking you. Cat leads, you follow. But rest assured, like a lion tamer, you'll be the hero of the neighborhood and every passing eye will swivel and heads will nod to acknowledge your training acumen.

Q **Why do cats rub against us?**

A When your cat rubs his head against your leg, he's doing it because he loves you. What . . . you don't rub up against the people you love? Hard to believe!

Your cat is definitely showing his affection for you, but he's also marking you as his property by putting his scent on you. Sebaceous glands at the base of your cat's hair follicles produce sebum, a substance that serves two purposes: coating the fur for protection and depositing scent on objects in the cat's environment.

These glands are most numerous around your cat's mouth and on the chin, lips, upper eyelids, on the top of the base of the tail, on the paw pads, and near his anus and genitals. If a cat rubs with his head (a behavior known as bunting) or any of these scent-loaded parts of his body, he's depositing both sebum and his own distinct scent on everything he touches. Call it pussy perfume, if you will.

Our pitiful noses can't detect these deposits – which is just as well – but other cats surely can. The message to other cats: mine! mine! mine!

Q Why won't my cat use the litter box?

A Honestly, we could write a book about this. Veterinarians and pet-care writers have dreams about these problems; in fact, we have nightmares about them.

For any pet-care professional, the number-one behavior problem for all cats is litter box avoidance. It's not even a contest. So at least if you're having these problems, you have lots of company.

Where to start? The first rule of solving a litter box problem: Whenever you have a problem – especially one that starts for no apparent reason – you need to rule out the possibility that your cat has a medical issue. (The second rule of solving a litter box problem: There is always a reason. It's just that sometimes the reason is apparent to your cat but not to you.) Urinary tract infections and diseases such as diabetes make consistent litter box use impossible for even the most well-intentioned cat. You cannot hope to get your cat using the box again until her health issues have been resolved.

If your cat checks out fine, you need to make sure everything about the box is to her liking. The third rule of solving a litter box problem: If the cat isn't happy, no one will be happy.

Here's what to look for:

Cleanliness. Cats are fastidious animals, and if the litter box is dirty, they look elsewhere for a place to go. Scoop the box frequently – twice a day, at least – and make sure it's completely scrubbed clean and aired out once a week. Toss out and replace the entire litter box once a year. Having an additional litter box may help, too; a good general rule is one litter box per cat per floor in your home, plus one. So if you have two cats and a two-story house, you'll need five litter boxes.

Box type and filler. Many choices people make to suit their own tastes conflict with the cat's sense of what's appropriate. A covered box may seem more pleasing to you, but your cat may think it's pretty rank inside – or scary. A box with high sides may be tough for your old or very small or rather portly cat to get in and out of. Scented litters may make you think the box smells fine, but your cat may disagree – not only is the box dirty, she reasons, but it's got this extra odor she can't abide. Start with the basics: a large box with unscented, clumping litter. Another great tip is to put out several litter boxes filled with several types of litter – a kind of 'waste test' – and let your cat choose the product she prefers. Give the brands your cat doesn't like to the local shelter and keep the extra litter boxes as handy replacements.

Location. Your cat's box should be away from her food and water, in a place she can get to easily and feel safe in. Consider a location from a cat's point of view: Choose a quiet spot where she can see what's coming at her. Would you like to go potty next to a rumbling washing machine? A cat doesn't want any surprises while she's in the box.

Make the area where your cat has had mistakes less attractive by cleaning it thoroughly with a pet-odor neutralizer (available from pet supply retailers). Discourage reuse by covering the area with foil, plastic sheeting, or plastic carpet runners with the pointy side facing up.

If all that doesn't work . . . go back to your veterinarian and get a referral to a feline behaviorist who can set up a specific program for you and your cat that will get her thinking inside the box again. Your vet may also need to prescribe medications for the transitional period. Pheromone products such as Feliway may help, too, and the behaviorist will show you how to use them.

And don't give up! Your cat is counting on you.

YOU'RE ASKING ME NOW?

Because there are so many environmental and behavioral factors, plus medical conditions, that can cause the litter box problems, and because they are so hard to resolve, every veterinarian dreads yet another query about how to get kitty to use the proper privy.

A friend of mine from St Louis holds the record for the most inappropriate 'inappropriate elimination' question of all time. Dr Dennis Cloud was in the hospital with a life-threatening illness. The patriarch of a big Catholic family, Dr Cloud was so sick that he remembers hearing his wife and her friends holding a prayer vigil in the hallway and that the priest had been contacted in case he had to deliver last rites.

Drifting in and out of consciousness, tubes everywhere, Dr Cloud was getting a glimpse of the light beyond when he was awakened by somebody calling his name and shaking him. Jesus?

No, it was a nurse who introduced herself by saying, 'Dr Cloud, do you remember me? I'm a client of yours. This probably isn't a very good time to ask you this, but my cat isn't using the litter box. Can you tell me what to do?'

Doc just shook his head, wondering if he was being punished by God. The last thing he was going to do on Earth was address one final cat box question? He thought for a few seconds about going toward the light, but in the end he went toward the litter. He motioned for the nurse to bring him the pen and paper on the nightstand and wrote out some toilet tips for her fat tabby.

Good Dr Cloud recovered and still practices veterinary medicine. And he still looks at the appointment book and grimaces when he reads the entering complaint: cat not using litter box.

— Dr Marty Becker

Q Whenever I go away, even for a weekend, my cat pees on my pillow. Why is he being so spiteful?

A Remember, cats aren't little people in fur coats — they're a completely different species. A lot of the motives people attribute to cats just aren't possible. Cats live in the here and now, and unlike some ex-spouses, revenge is not part of who they are.

Behaviors like urinating outside the litter box, scratching and knocking your things off the dresser . . . well, they are natural, normal behaviors, part of every cat's DNA. Cats who do that stuff are just being cats. The fact that we'd rather they didn't is just a compatibility issue between felines and humans.

Cats have no idea a behavior is 'bad' until you teach them in terms a cat can clearly understand. And they definitely don't urinate on your pillow because they're mad at you for leaving them; they urinate because they're stressed about being alone and pouring their personal scent over something that smells strongly of you is very comforting to a cat. Your cat misses you, and this is his way of coping.

Other factors may also be in play: Perhaps the box has become a minefield of wet clumps and kitty poops in your absence – unfit for any self-respecting cat.

Spite? That's just too complicated for cats, who tend to have a more simple range of emotions, like fear . . . and joy. Their ability to live so simply and so joyfully is, after all, one of the reasons we love sharing our lives with them.

Studies have shown that stress alone can alter the pH of a cat's urine, causing bladder irritations that can lead to litter box avoidance.

Q *Can you really teach a cat to use the toilet? Not a litter box, I really mean a toilet!*

A If you can manage to put down this book (although why would you want to?) and go to the Internet, we promise you will find no fewer than half a dozen videos of cats precariously perched on a toilet seat, their faces a model of life-or-death concentration as they squat precariously on the edge, the way other cats would in a litter box.

We will also promise that cats will not be so considerate as to flush. Although human nature being what it is, if some inventor hasn't already figured out some electronic-eye gizmo similar to those used on automatic litter boxes to flush the toilet when the cat is through . . . well, we would be extremely disappointed. (And if someone reads this and does invent such a contraption, we demand 10 percent of all future earnings for giving you the idea. You'll be hearing from our attorneys.)

We also promise that cats are not picky about spraying on the seat. As far as we're concerned, that is reason enough not to share a toilet with a cat.

So. Cats. Toilets. Possible? Sure. Likely? Not all that much, in our opinion. The position is just too precarious and uncomfortable to convince a cat to keep at it.

In fact, in our opinion, based on nearly fifty years combined of giving pet-care advice, you should be very, very happy if your cat uses the litter box without fail – and leave it at that.

Cats bury their waste to hide evidence of their presence from predators and avoid territorial turf battles with other cats.

Q Does neutering stop a cat from spraying?

A If a cat is neutered before sexual maturity, the procedure will reduce the chance that he'll ever start marking territory with urine. If he's neutered after sexual maturity and after he starts spraying, there's still a great chance that he'll stop, but the odds are not as good. And finally, for some cats, neutering has no effect on spraying. (For the record, even some females spray.)

Spraying can be a complicated behavior to resolve. Contrary to common belief, it's a completely different problem from a cat who won't use the litter box. If your cat's a persistent, chronic sprayer, he'll need to be neutered (if he's not already), and you should ask your veterinarian for a referral to a feline behaviorist who can recommend medication (for the cat, not for you) and work on behavioral modification (ditto), and other strategies that may turn the smelly tide.

Q *Why do cats get abscesses? I swear, I am always at the veterinarian with my cat all spring and summer, having him treated.*

A Nearly every free-roaming cat will one day need to see a veterinarian to have an abscess treated — surgically opened, flushed clean of debris, and sometimes temporarily held open by drains to let the wound heal with the help of time and some strong antibiotics. Sound awful? It is.

The good news is that an abscess is one of those health problems that can usually be prevented by keeping a cat indoors. That's because this common feline health problem is often the result of a puncture wound, specifically a bite from another cat during a fight over territory or mates (yes, that's what cats fight about!).

A cat's mouth is a nasty mix of bacteria, and once that bacteria gets punched into another cat's body, the result will probably be an abscess. Think about it: A bunch of bacteria is injected with two bacteria-laden hypodermic needles (the cat's fang teeth) into a perfect incubator (another cat's 101-degree-plus body). The only possible outcome is infection.

The best way to prevent your cat from getting a bite-wound abscess is to neuter him to reduce his desire to fight (remember what we just said cats fight about?) and, preferably, keep him indoors.

The bacteria in a cat's mouth is also why even relatively minor cat bites can become serious medical issues for humans, leading to hospitalization in some cases. Any time you're bitten or scratched by an animal, you should wash it out immediately with soap and water and have the wound checked by a doctor.

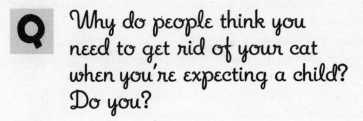

Q

Why do people think you need to get rid of your cat when you're expecting a child? Do you?

A Absolutely not! Cats are not a danger to pregnant women or to new babies.

Anyone who has ever been expecting has heard the well-intended advice that when a baby is on the way, a cat must go. There are two reasons for this: one with a legitimate kernel of concern, the other with not even a popcorn of validity.

First, the real concern. Toxoplasmosis, a disease caused by a microscopic creature that most of us have already been exposed to, can give infected people (and cats) flulike symptoms that usually go away on their own. But if a fetus is exposed during the first trimester of pregnancy, severe birth defects can be the result. Improper handling of cat feces is one way to be exposed to toxoplasmosis; improper handling of meat is another. So is gardening in infected soil. In fact, the number of cases caused by improper handling of meat far outweigh exposure from the other two.

Still, cats are the ideal host for the toxoplasmosis organism, and they are the only animals to shed the infective organisms in their feces. This dubious distinction has given them a bad rap. In fact, an infected cat is only capable of passing on the disease while she's in the throes of an acute infection – which is seven to ten days of her entire life. And the feces eliminated by a cat carrying toxoplasmosis requires anywhere from one to five days to become actively infectious. That means all you have to do is scoop all feces from the litter box and dispose of it within twenty-four hours to avoid becoming infected.

But even if you didn't scoop that frequently, to acquire the infection you'd have to touch the feces and then touch an opening in your body without first washing your hands. How disgusting does this sound?

So although the danger is real, the risks can be significantly reduced by washing your hands right after scooping the box, wearing rubber gloves when you scoop, or, best of all, simply asking a family member to do all the scooping while you're pregnant. And since cats are really not the big-risk sources of this infection, you'll have to wear gloves while gardening and practice safe meat-handling techniques, too. Any woman who's expecting should be able to get information on precautions from her doctor; if not, several medical, veterinary and national humane society Web sites offer guidance.

Second, the myth we're happy to debunk: Cats do not cause sudden infant death syndrome or otherwise attempt to 'suck the breath' from infants. You can see how such an idea may have been started, though. A baby, tragically found dead; a cat, who may have been curious about the infant, perhaps out of friendliness or intrigued by the smell of spit-up milk or death, found licking the baby's lips. Could the cat have been responsible? People always have a need to find explanations for their losses, and we can think of no loss more profound than that of a child, especially an apparently healthy one.

But cats are not a danger to infants, and there's no need to find a new home for yours when you're expecting. Of course, all interactions between pets and young children should be supervised, but that's just common sense. It's also easy to cover the crib with a net (premade ones are available at baby supply stores) to keep the cat out when you're not able to watch closely.

Q Can cats tell time?

A When it suits them, absolutely. If you feed your cat every day precisely at 6 p.m., you're soon going to find your cat underfoot and crying for attention at 5:45 p.m. Which means you can put the alarm clock you got as a wedding present in the garage sale pile.

Cats also know when you're coming home and have usually managed to end their sixty-second catnap of the day to present themselves at the front door or on the kitchen counter, tail up and delighted to see you.

So don't be late or they'll greet you with their paws on their hips, eyes narrowed, lips turned down with a look that says, 'Where have you been?'

Q Can you teach a cat tricks?

A Some people point to the dog's ability to associate behaviors with words as proof that dogs are smarter than cats. And some people argue that the cat's apparent disinterest in doing tricks for our amusement marks feline intelligence as far, far more advanced than the canine variety.

Well guess what? You can teach an old cat new tricks. But there has to be something in it for the cat. And that something is going to be food – really, really tasty tidbits.

You can teach a cat to sit, for example, by holding a favorite treat over a cat's head and saying 'sit' while you move the treat back. To watch it, the cat must sit down. When his backside hits the ground, kitty gets the yummy for his tummy.

This kind of training is based on a principle called operant conditioning, which basically says that if an animal is rewarded for doing something, he's likely to do it again to try to get another reward. It's the principle behind clicker training, in which the treat is associated with the sound of a children's toy that makes a small clicking noise. Desired behavior, click, treat. Simple!

Once you get the hang of it – and it's not that hard – using a clicker to teach tricks is entertaining for both you and your cat. And there's no end to what you can do. In fact, our friend Steve

Dale, another syndicated pet-care columnist, trained his cat Ricky to play a toy piano. (Ricky played only free jazz. Were you expecting Mozart?) Ricky passed away, and Steve is now training another cat using a clicker.

Behaviorist Karen Pryor was one of the first to bring clicker training from the world of marine mammal training to pet training, and her Web site, www.clickertraining.com, is the best resource for starting out.

Q Why do cats like to drink running water?

A Why do you?

Standing water often isn't safe, and animals instinctively know this. (Perhaps because over the generations animals who didn't know this didn't live long enough to reproduce.) Running water is a better bet to not be contaminated (in theory, anyway), and it's often cooler as well. Greater oxygenation may also make the water taste better. A more appealing prospect all around, and cats know it.

Some cats are so enamored of running water that they've trained their owners to turn on the tap for them. Faced with an untrainable owner, some cats learn to turn on the tap by themselves.

Because the appeal of running water is so great, veterinarians often suggest that older cats or cats who have a health condition that can cause them to be underhydrated be given a feline water fountain – basically, a water dish that is constantly recycling, oxygenating and filtering itself – so they always have access to clean, fresh, running water. This will often encourage cats to drink more.

Q Are all kittens born with blue eyes?

A Cats have many different eye colors as adults – all beautiful, in our opinion – but at birth, all kittens have baby blues. If their eyes change color, it generally occurs at four to five weeks of age. They'll start to darken as natural pigments are deposited in the iris.

Cats with points – light body color and dark markings on the ears, face mask, legs and tail, like the Siamese – will keep those blue eyes. White cats will have blue, green, gold or copper eyes – or one of each. Other cats will have green, gold or copper eyes, and those baby blues will change as they leave infancy behind.

Kittens open their eyes at seven to ten days but can't hear until they're about fourteen days old.

Q Do cats get 'doggy' breath?

A You're lucky your cat doesn't claw you for the insult. No, cats don't get doggy breath, but they do have their own set of dental issues that can lead to kitty breath – also known as tuna breath. While periodontal disease is a big problem in dogs, in cats cavities are not uncommon. Technically called feline oral resorptive lesions, they eat through a cat's healthy teeth and can cause great pain. Veterinarians who specialize in dentistry say up to half of all cats show signs of these dental problems by the age of four – although so far they're not really sure why.

The best way to deal with feline dental problems is prevention. (Why are you surprised? It's the best way to deal with your own dental problems.) Regularly brushing or wiping the teeth with treated wipes (or even plain gauze) can help keep dental problems from developing. Cats who become accustomed to having their teeth cleaned as kittens don't mind it at all – or at least, they don't mind as much. And even adult cats can usually be trained to tolerate brushing.

In addition to at-home care, a thorough dental exam should be part of your cat's wellness check by your veterinarian, who may suggest regular cleanings under anesthesia to fix little problems before they become big ones.

If your cat does have kitty breath, by the way, it may be a

problem with his teeth and gums, or it may be a symptom of another health problem. A stinky mouth is not normal for any pet and should not be left untreated!

Never, ever use toothpaste made for humans to brush your cat's teeth. The fluoride is not good for cats, and the toothpaste itself is made to spit out, which a cat can't do. Plus, have you ever seen a cat crave a flavor like mint? Stick with the cat toothpastes, in yummy flavors like shrimp and chicken.

WHY LIVE TV AND PETS DON'T ALWAYS MIX

I've been the resident veterinarian on ABC-TV's *Good Morning, America* for almost a decade. While I've learned to be a lot less nervous over the years, it's still hard to be confident, competent and compassionate for four or five minutes of live television, especially when your furry co-stars don't always cooperate.

The most terrifying moment I've faced on television was when I was doing a live segment with Diane Sawyer about brushing your pet's teeth. She was holding a little dog, and I had movie critic Joel Siegel's cat in my lap.

Before the segment started, the cat started squirming. Wanting to maintain the image of the gentle doctor, I didn't want to physically restrain the cat — as any veterinarian would in an ordinary exam room. I could see the producer counting us down with his fingers to go live: 10, 9, 8 . . .

Suddenly, at about the count of 2, the cat went limp in my arms. I panicked. Had I unknowingly had my hands around his neck and starved the poor animal of oxygen? While Diane was introducing the segment and the cameras were off me, I stole a glance at the cat and was relieved to see him sitting calmly in my lap. Whew!

We talked about how dental disease is the most commonly diagnosed problem in veterinary medicine. We talked about the health risks of poor oral health and how owners can keep their pets' teeth and gums in great shape. I talked about special pet toothpastes and toothbrushes, and Diane cocked her head like an inquisitive cat.

'Marty, you mean you should brush your cat's teeth?' she asked. 'Show me how!'

My heart stopped, knowing this was not something to try on live television with a nervous cat I'd just met. Talk about risky business! But with Diane, three cameras, the studio audience and proud Papa Siegel just off to the side all staring at me, I couldn't say no. I picked up the toothbrush from the table, reached for the cat, who kindly opened his mouth for me, and started brushing his teeth.

Diane was incredulous. 'I can't believe he lets you brush his teeth!' she said.

Truth is, neither could I!

When the segment was over, the executive producer walked over. 'Marty, that was a great segment,' he said. 'You really have a way with animals.'

Knowing how close I had been to disaster just minutes before, I simply smiled, nodded and said, 'Yeah I do.'

But really, some days you just get lucky.

— Dr Marty Becker

Q My veterinarian says my cat needs to have her teeth cleaned, but this means anesthesia. Is putting my cat under really safe?

 Anesthesia is common in veterinary medicine, but there are still many misconceptions about its use, especially in older animals.

Yes, it's true that no anesthesia is without risks. It's also true that in the hands of a good veterinarian and staff, anesthesia has become a very safe procedure. The risks are so low that, with few exceptions, you should not be dissuaded from pursuing necessary preventive or other procedures for your cat. In most cases, the risks of not doing the procedure (such as pulling infected teeth) far outweigh the risks of knocking your pet out so that she can be treated safely and without pain. Imagine trying to clean a cat's teeth while she's wide awake!

The risks can be greatly minimized by taking a thorough health history and doing a physical examination and a few basic tests beforehand, including a laboratory evaluation of blood and urine, and possibly a chest X-ray. Although these tests add to the cost of a procedure, they enable your veterinarian to fully understand the health status of your cat before anesthetizing her. These are the same kinds of tests you would want for any member of your family who was going under anesthesia.

Your veterinarian is especially interested in looking at the functioning of your cat's liver and kidneys, because they are responsible for metabolizing many of the anesthetic agents and are, in large part, the barometer of whether your cat can be routinely anesthetized or needs special precautions. During the procedure, placing an IV catheter and administering fluids, monitoring the heart and body temperature, and measuring oxygen levels and blood pressure can further add to the safety of the anesthesia.

The final piece in keeping your cat safe is yours. Make sure you follow your veterinarian's instructions to the letter, both before and after any procedure that requires anesthesia. And if you have questions or concerns, ask and keep asking until they are addressed.

Q Why do cats chatter when they see a bird out the window?

A Chattering is an involuntary reaction of a cat who sees something she wants very badly, such as a fluttering bird or a feline enemy, but can't get to for some reason, such as being on one side of the window when the bird or other cat is visible.

If the keyed-up cat could pop her knuckles or chew gum to let out that extra energy, she would.

Q My cat seems to enjoy watching her reflection in the mirror. Does she know she's looking at herself?

A Like many predators, cats are very quick to notice movement, which is why they'll often react to their own image in a mirror. It's unlikely that they recognize the image as themselves, but may briefly react as if they've seen another cat. But since that 'other cat' doesn't have any smell, they eventually decide there's nothing to it. Cats know their world first by the way it smells, and next by the way it sounds. Cats in the mirror just don't cut it.

Initial encounters between pets and mirrors can be pretty hilarious, though, so if you have a new kitten, have the video camera close at hand because you may have something to send to *You've Been Framed*.

This attraction to motion is also why some cats are intrigued by television – which goes a step better than the mirror, adding sound to images. For some cats, this is enough to keep their attention, at least for a while. This is especially true if the programming is geared to cats, with images of birds and rodents with a scratchy, squeaky soundtrack to match. Several companies now sell DVDs just for cats, designed to keep the animals engaged while owners are at work. There's even a radio station just for pets in California.

All eyes have cells called rods and cones. Rods react to changing intensities of light, while cones react to color. A cat's eyes have more rods than we have, and fewer cones. This means that while we have better color vision, a cat can detect motion better.

Q *Why do cats chase the light from a laser pointer?*

A All healthy cats find moving objects irresistible. It's play, but then again, all play is really about keeping their hunting skills sharp – even for those cats who will never have to worry about where their next meal is coming from.

Laser pointers didn't start out as cat toys, of course, but rather as modern-day office tools, used to draw attention to some extra special number being projected on a screen. We suppose it was during one of those endless and truly pointless PowerPoint presentations that some daydreamer in the audience thought, 'Hey, I bet my cat would chase that little dot of light.'

Having sat through more than our share of such meetings, we hope that person immediately went home and started her own business, quit her boring job, and is now sipping margaritas on the veranda of her beach house . . . with her cat, of course!

Don't be disappointed if your cat finds the laser pointer interesting for exactly one pounce, though. Some cats are more literal than others, and once they discover that there is nothing to actually grab and bite, they find that little red dot to be a big waste of energy.

Oh, and because we know you're wondering: Don't let the kids play with the laser pointer unless you're certain they're old enough and responsible enough not to point the light in the cat's eyes (or their siblings').

And don't run with scissors. We mean it.

FREEBIE TOYS CATS LOVE

Catnip mice, cat 'fishing poles,' laser pointers, and more — you can have a blast spending money on toys to keep your cat suitably amused. But you can also supplement those fun purchases with playthings that won't cost you a dime.

Back in the days when smoking was more socially acceptable, my dad (a pack-a-day man) used to entertain our cats by wadding up empty cigarette packs and sending them skittering across the linoleum floor of our kitchen, with the cats in hot pursuit. It was the crunchy, crinkly sound they loved, and you can get that from a plain old piece of paper.

Cats can also have a blast with corks from champagne or wine bottles, the retainer rings off plastic milk jugs, paper grocery bags and cardboard boxes.

— Gina Spadafori

Q Why does my cat attack me when he sees another cat outside the window?

A Have you ever had a really bad day at the office, come home and snapped at your mate? That's roughly what's happening when a frustrated indoor cat attacks another pet or person inside the house because they're worked up over an animal on the other side of the glass. It's called redirected aggression, and it can be accompanied by other signs of frustration from the indoor cat, such as urine spraying.

Not fair, is it? In fact, it can be downright scary.

Cats are very territorial and don't appreciate seeing other cats on what they view as their turf. In an area with free-roaming cats, the animals work out their territory with scent marking, visual marking (claw marks) and, occasionally, fighting. But when a cat is kept indoors, he doesn't have a chance to mark or otherwise defend his yard from cats who trot through as if they own the place. It would be like one gang member spray painting gang colors or doing drive-bys in an opposing gang's 'hood, and the opposing gang member is forced to watch it all from a living-room window without responding.

A motion-detector sprinkler may keep stray cats out of your

yard. And if there's one window that seems to be the perfect vantage point for your indoor cat to see the marauding members of the feline gang, you might think about keeping the blinds closed or closing off that room. And of course, keep an eye on your cat: If he's agitated, he's best avoided until the stranger is gone and your kitty calms down. Products with pheromones (such as Feliway) may also help calm the indoor cat.

Q What's the biggest breed of cat? The smallest?

A The weight range of a 'normal' cat of unrecorded parentage – what our British friends so endearingly call a moggie – is between seven and twelve pounds. Some breeds of cat routinely weigh a few pounds more, without an ounce of fat on them. Among the heaviest breeds are Norwegian forest cats (who can weigh seven to twenty pounds), Maine coon cats (seven to twenty-two pounds), ragdolls (ten to twenty pounds), Siberians (ten to twenty pounds) and Turkish Vans (seven to nineteen pounds).

The Singapura is the smallest breed of cat, with females as tiny as four pounds (although they can get as big as five, and the males can weigh up to seven pounds). The Cornish rex, Devon rex, and Japanese bobtail are also feline featherweights, weighing in at about six to nine pounds.

Q What's the best way to stop a cat fight?

A Not to be flip about it, but the best way to keep cats from mixing it up is to never let a fight get started. You can do this in a general way by keeping your cat inside so she won't be involved in neighborhood territory skirmishes.

If cats – yours or the neighbor's – are going at it in your yard, the tried-and-true method is to turn the hose on them. Yes, it will separate the combatants. No, it's not a nice thing to do. But all things considered, being sprayed with water is far better than getting an abscess (or worse!) from a bite wound.

In your house, if you see your cats revving up for a fight with a low-pitched 'rooowwwrrr' accompanied by dirty looks, make a loud noise. They'll look at you as if you're crazy, but they'll stop looking at each other with malicious intent.

Housemate cats who are chronically battling may need to be separated temporarily – or for good; many a household has cats who live upstairs and other cats who live downstairs, with the staircase as a kind of No Cats Zone.

Whatever you do, don't try to physically separate the combatants. You will get hurt!

Q Why do cats bring dead mice and birds into the house?

A Lovers bring chocolates, cats bring mice. We all have our own way of saying, 'I love you.' And consider this: Cats don't bring you any old dead mice. No! These are mice they have hunted and killed themselves, only the best for you, baby!

There's something about the thrill of the hunt that stirs even the best-fed cat to stalk, chase and pounce. But only love will inspire her to share.

If you're not understanding enough to realize that the occasional headless mouse in bed is a gift of true respect and admiration – not to mention a tasty treat your cat wants you to eat! – well, we're not sure you're truly cat-lover material.

Dead critters are bad enough, of course, but what about those cats who bring in the mortally wounded? Then you have a cat who really, really loves you. Not only is she making sure you don't starve, but she's trying her best to make sure you understand how to feed yourself – and are entertained as well. It's your turn to play with the prey. Don't you just love a cat who shares her toys?

Your mother taught you to say thank you, didn't she? Now give your cat its just rewards by smiling and making a big deal out of the carcass. But before you get rid of that mouse or finch, put some gloves on. You never know what vile disease that critter may be harboring.

Q **Will putting a bell on a cat's collar really protect birds from being killed?**

A Probably not. In fact, some experts have observed that a cat with a bell on her collar – like a yo-yo dieter headed for the cookie jar – can learn to stalk her prey without ever making the bell sound. A cat who's determined to hunt will hunt, given the opportunity – and she will be successful.

Groups such as the Audubon Society are very much against free-roaming cats, whether they're pets given access to the outside or former pets turned out who are living as best they can. Studies have shown that cats do kill their fair share of birds, but they also kill a lot of animals that are neither endangered nor desired, such as mice and rats.

People who advocate for the humane handling of feral cat colonies argue that blaming the decline in songbirds on cats is a bit of a 'glass house' situation. The biggest threats to all species are habitat destruction and pollution. Cats have nothing to do with those problems. In fact, in the case of birds, more die by flying into tall glass buildings than are killed by cats.

The debate will rage on, no doubt. In the meantime, if you want to keep your cat from hunting, keep her inside. It's safer for her, anyway.

A cat has a pouncing average that a major league baseball player would envy. About one pounce in three ends up with dinner! How do cats learn to hunt? All that crazy kitten play, pouncing on bugs and chasing dust balls, is practice for grown-up hunting. Mom helps, too. Cats have a genetic predisposition to kill things (after all, cats are carnivores), but they also learn from watching Mom, who teaches them how to whip up a dish of Mice-A-Roni from something the cat dragged in.

Q *Do cats get colds? Can we catch them from our cats or give cats our colds?*

A Cats do get common upper respiratory infections. They're usually caused by viruses, although just as with the viruses that make us miserable, secondary bacterial infections can play a role.

Upper respiratory infections are very contagious, but only to other cats. The viruses that love to invade us are not interested in cats, and vice versa. In other words, you can't catch a cold from your cat, and your cat can't catch a cold from you.

Q *How can I keep my cat from unrolling the toilet paper?*

A Keep the bathroom door closed. (Don't you love how we always have the easy answers?)

Of course, the chances of the bathroom door remaining closed diminish as the number of people in the household increases; it's one of the immutable laws of nature. And if you have kids in the house, forget about it!

Instead, you can try to hang the paper so it unrolls from underneath instead of over the top. That might take care of the problem. Of course, that solution also depends on the cooperation of a family that might not even be capable of putting up a new roll when the old one is done. Plus, some cats just see that as a more challenging game – but not an impossible one.

If you really, really have a problem with your cat playing with the toilet paper, look in the back of cat magazines or home-notion catalogs for plastic shields that mount on the wall and fit over the top of the roll.

And no, we can't help you get your kids to squeeze the toothpaste tube from the end or get the cat to lower the toilet seat to cover for the males who conveniently forget to.

Q *I've heard you can read a cat's thoughts just by looking at his tail. Is that true?*

 A Nobody can read the feline mind. But it's not a tall tale that you can tell a lot from looking at your cat's tail.

Think of a cat's tail as instant messaging with a kicker!

You can tell that you're a few seconds away from being introduced to a cat's claws, for one thing! When you're petting a cat who enjoys the attention – at least for the moment – the tail will move languidly. When a cat's getting to the limit of his tolerance for attention, the tail tip will flip rapidly in annoyance. The more annoyed the cat, the more of the tail will swish rapidly. This is like a NASCAR flagman furiously waving the caution flag at a race. This is a cat who needs to be left alone!

On the other hand, a cat can also express friendliness and good-natured curiosity with his tail. A relaxed, happy cat – or one who's expecting you to open a can of food very soon – will have his tail as upright as a flagpole.

When a cat is tracking something interesting, his tail will be held low, twitching erratically. Fear or anger will bring out the 'Halloween tail' – stuck out and puffed up. That's another cat who needs to be left alone. If you don't heed the tale of the tail, tell your partner to start the car because you'll soon be going to the emergency room to have your wounds treated!

Cats are the only species that can hold their tails vertically while walking.

Q Is it really safe for cats to get 'high' on catnip?

A Here's one of the real advantages of being feline. You can get, like, totally, totally high, and it's . . . um . . . cool, cat. Totally fur out.

It's not as if cats drive, have to show up for work or are faced with huge personal decisions, such as how to invest their savings. Mostly, cats have to decide if they'd rather nap in the chair or on the couch, or play with the mousie toy or the little ball. And if those decisions must wait awhile, well, what difference does it make?

In short: Let your cat have all the catnip he wants. The fresher the better, so keep some growing in a protected place – protected from your cat that is – and snip off bits to slip into cat toys or rub on the cat tree.

Not all cats like catnip. The ability to appreciate the herb is genetic, with slightly more cats in the fan club than not. These hardwired preferences aren't immediately apparent, though, since kittens under the age of three months don't react to catnip at all.

Among those cats who do like catnip, you'll find two basic kinds of reactions: Your cat may turn into

either a lazy drunk or a wired-up crazy. Credit a substance called nepetalactone, a volatile oil that is found in the leaves and stems and causes the mood-altering behavior. It's released when you crush the leaves, so crunch up the catnip to release that intoxicating aroma before offering it to your cat.

Q *Why is it a cat can climb up a tree but sometimes can't get down?*

A Cat claws are designed to move a cat forward, anchoring her as she propels herself. If that forward direction is up a tree, it's difficult to head back down. Instead, the gracefully powerful movement of a cat heading up a tree is counterbalanced by the crashing and (if she's lucky) controlled free fall she'll use to get down.

Most cats do find their way back down, of course, which is a good thing these days. With municipal budgets being what they are, few fire departments are allowed to respond to 'cat stuck in tree' calls anymore.

We don't recommend that you get out that tall ladder, either. You have a better chance of getting seriously hurt while reaching for a scared cat – and scared cats aren't safe to handle, even if they're yours – than your cat does of getting injured when she decides it's time to head down for dinner. You may be able to whet her appetite by opening a can of tuna, salmon or mackerel and letting the wonderful fishy smell drift upward.

GETTING HIGH FOR MY CAT

I have never personally seen a cat skeleton in a tree and I have never heard of one being found there. So it's always been my contention that cats who are 'stuck' in trees will eventually find a way to get themselves down — on their own.

That is, until my own cat was, shall we say, 'detained' up a tree for five days. By then, I swore she was close to going to the highest perch — heaven. So against my better judgment and my advice to others in newspaper columns, I rescued her, alone, using a 30-foot ladder in a snowstorm. The things you do for love!

— Dr Marty Becker

Q *Are collars dangerous for cats?*

A Yes they are – if you leave them off. Anyone who works in an animal shelter will tell you that a lot of cats who clearly belong back with their families never go home again because there's no way to tell where home is.

People don't like to put collars on their cats because they're afraid their pets will get snagged and won't be able to wriggle free. We say: Get a collar with an elastic insert that will let your cat slip out of it if snagged. And then put an ID tag on the collar.

While we're on the subject, make an appointment to get your cat permanently identified with a microchip, a device the size of a grain of rice that's implanted beneath the skin over the shoulders and can be read using a special device. If your cat does slip his collar and ends up in a shelter or is taken to a veterinary hospital, a microchip may get him home again.

Q What's the best way to hold a cat?

A That depends on the cat's state of mind. If you're looking at a cat who's scared or angry, the best way to hold her is to get someone else to do it! If you must get your cat under control, you can scruff her: Take a firm hold on the loose skin at the nape of the neck — and we do mean firm, like a mama cat who means business!

Otherwise, the best way to pick up your cat is to make sure you're not surprising her when you do so. Say something to get her attention, then scoop her under the midsection and then hold her under the chest with one hand while your other hand supports her hind end. Better still, let her chest rest against yours while you support her rump from below.

If you're holding a cat who's suddenly in a panic, the best thing you can do is let go. Once a cat reaches that flight-or-fight threshold, you do not want to be the thing she's trying to defeat or run away from. Razor-sharp claws and teeth like hypodermic needles are nothing to mess with. Let go!

Q Why are cats so noisy when they're mating?

A When it comes to sex, cats don't spend much time on foreplay, afterplay or much play at all. Cat sex is quick and nasty . . . and yes, it's noisy.

Feline copulation starts when the female lets the male know she's open to his advances – reluctantly so, it would appear, since he approaches her cautiously, looking out lest her claws rake him somewhere, including the . . . well, never mind.

When he gets close enough, he doesn't want to give her a chance to change her mind. So he grabs the female's neck for about 16 seconds while maneuvering himself into position, which can take about another 107 seconds. Thrusting and ejaculation? A whole 20 seconds.

If all goes well, the mating process is over in less than 3 minutes – and not a second too soon for either of the participants.

During copulation, the female will scream because the male has barbs on his penis – yes, we said barbs – and attempt to break free by rolling or striking at the male with her claws. After it's all over, the male runs off to brag about his prowess (or lick his wounds), and the female has a so-called 'after reaction' where she'll roll or thrash around like a fish out of water and clean herself. This behavior may last up to 10 minutes before she's ready to go again.

Yes, we said again. The interval between matings may be as short as 5 minutes or as long as 30 minutes, and the female may allow up to 30 matings and isn't at all picky about which male is next. In this hotel, we rent by the minute, so take a number, pal.

As hair-raising as this may seem to us relatively staid humans, all this . . . uh . . . catting around has survival advantages. (You haven't noticed any shortage of cats, have you?) That's because the female is an induced ovulator, which means the very act of mating causes her to produce eggs. Without all that stimulation, there would be no eggs for the male to fertilize.

THE BIRDS, THE BEES . . . AND THE CATS

Growing up in rural southern Idaho at a time when spaying and neutering barn cats was unheard of, this veterinarian-to-be got one of the most visible and certainly most vocal lessons in the birds and the bees. No, Dad didn't take me aside for a nervous talk, and I didn't read the articles in the magazines under the mattress of a friend's college-bound brother.

My earliest sex education was courtesy of the barn cats who were mating right under my bedroom window.

Duke (named after John Wayne, of course) was a big, black, longhaired tom who lived in the shadows of our farm. I remember his most distinctive features were big jowls like the Godfather and a thick neck that made him look a little like a wrestler. His mistress that night was Punkin, the orange tabby barn cat who would sit on her haunches to drink milk arching across the barn straight from a cow's teat.

Looking and sounding to me more like a brawl than a breeding — with fur flying, vocal cords stretched like piano wires and teeth clamping — the actual mating took only a few seconds to complete.

In retrospect, the courtship between Duke and Punkin was certainly more leisurely, taking place in a complex ballet of behavior in and out of the farm buildings and haystacks, and lasting a few hours. When it comes to sex, the male cat (tom) and female cat (queen) are romantically shackled and shaped by genetic and biological patterns forged over millennia.
                                                    — Dr Marty Becker

Q My cat is neutered and I never see his penis. Is that what the vet cut off?

A Absolutely not! Your cat's testicles were removed. His penis is still there.

In the world of animal appendages, male cats may take the prize for the weirdest wedding tackle. Unlike most species, where the angle of the dangle is there for the whole world to see, a male cat's most important organ is not easily visible. But if you know where to look – between the back legs and close to the very back – you'll find the relaxed penis pointed down and back.

Put another way, if a cat's nose is pointing north, his penis is pointing south. Not that there's much to be pointing with: The average cat's penis is a little less than half an inch long – about the same size as a pencil eraser.

Something else odd about a cat's penis: It's equipped with barbs – about 120 to 150 of them arranged in six to eight rows. The barbs start to appear at around twelve weeks of age and are fully developed by puberty. In appearance they resemble the bumps on the surface of a cat's tongue, and their purpose is to trigger a reaction in the female that causes her hormones to make her ovulate. All together now, 'OUCH!'

Not the best arrangement, in our opinion, but certainly a successful one, as far as cats are concerned.

In neutered cats, by the way, those barbs disappear within about six weeks.

Male cats have a tiny bone in the penis, called the os penis. So they really do get a 'boner'.

Q *Is there any way I can tell if my cat is pregnant? How long does a feline pregnancy last?*

A Feline pregnancy lasts about sixty-six days from ovulation. If you're exceptionally observant, you may notice your cat's nipples changing colors fairly early in the pregnancy – veterinarians call this 'pinking up.'

Your veterinarian can confirm pregnancy in a couple of ways. As early as twenty days on, a really good veterinarian may be able to feel the kittens developing (they feel like a little string of pearls). It's not foolproof, but an experienced veterinarian can be pretty good at 'palpating' for the kittens.

Going with technology, ultrasound will reveal kittens starting at about twenty days into the pregnancy. A pregnancy test can confirm the diagnosis about halfway through, at which point you might be getting some suspicions about your cat's gradual trend toward roundness.

And finally, an X-ray at about forty-five days will show not only the presence of kittens, but will enable you to count them.

While reputable breeders may avail themselves of all these options as well as top prenatal care, the fact is that for many people, the first indication that the cat they adopted is pregnant is when she gives birth in the sock drawer. Whoops!

Every kitten has only one mother and one father. But in every litter there may be kittens with different dads, because one female may mate with several males. And that's a good thing: Any increase in genetic diversity and the potential for a successful pregnancy also increases the chances of survival of the species.

Q *Which is the more prolific breeder, rabbits or cats?*

A There's average, and then there's extraordinary. A female cat with good access to males who gets an early start in the breeding season (February to September) will probably be able to raise three litters of kittens per year. Litter sizes vary from one kitten to ten; the number of yarn-divers born is typically smaller in young and old animals and largest when the mother cat is a youthful three to four years of age. Add it all up, and a busy mother can crank out 50 to 150 kittens in her lifetime.

And those kittens can do the same, and their kittens, and their kittens, and so on. You can see how it all adds up.

Still, the rabbit's reputation as a breeding machine is well deserved. Rabbits can produce six or more litters a year, with each litter containing five to eight offspring. Rabbits are constantly pregnant throughout the breeding season, which also runs from February to September. If you are math challenged, that's about thirty to fifty-six baby bunnies per year. So in the sheer numbers department, rabbits win.

Cats have fewer litters per year because their pregnancy is so much longer (about sixty-six days for cats versus thirty days for rabbits), and the mother cat must invest more time in raising the kittens.

Not that cats aren't trying to keep up. The book *Cats Out of the Bag* says that the oldest known cat to have kittens was Kitty, who gave birth to twins in 1987 at the age of thirty. They were her 217th and 218th kittens!

WHAT'S WRONG WITH MY CAT?

One of the best things about being a pet-care columnist is when you can stop someone from worrying about a pet with just a few words of explanation.

Every year I hear from frantic readers who are worried that something's seriously wrong with their half-grown female cat. She won't stop crying. She won't stop yowling. She is writhing around on the carpet as if she just had her tail slammed in the door.

I'm always happy to set these owners' minds at ease: Their cat isn't injured; she's in heat.

To put it simply: Once a female cat reaches sexual maturity, she's pretty much in heat any time she's not pregnant. And she's back in heat not long after giving birth.

A female cat in heat may accept several males, resulting in kittens from the same litter having different fathers. (The technical term for this is superfecundity; the street expression is 'catting around.') Lactation (production of milk) does not suppress the heat cycle. Cats who are actively nursing kittens can come into heat as soon as two weeks after giving birth.

Even being pregnant doesn't necessarily suppress the heat cycle; 10 percent of female cats come into heat between the third and sixth week of pregnancy. It's rare but possible for a cat to be carrying fetuses of different ages, resulting from separate matings in different heat cycles. (The scientific term for this is superfetation; the street lingo is 'felicitous feline.')

In other words, a female cat is in constant 'she's gotta have it' mode. Which is why, for the sanity of cat and human alike, there's no time like the present to get that cat spayed. (And don't forget the boys, because tom cats who mark their territory like graffiti artists, spraying urine rather than paint, aren't much fun to live with, either!)

— Gina Spadafori

Q *Why do cats think it's nice to be kneaded?*

A Cat lovers all know the special paw motions of a happy cat in the lap, although no one seems to agree on what to call this pleasurable bit of body language. Call it 'making biscuits' or 'kneading,' the message is the same: affection and trust. Like a hug.

Making biscuits is a holdover from kittenhood. When cats are babies, they move their paws against their mother's side when nursing. When your cat does this to you, he's telling you he considers you to be just like his mother – purring and kneading is a demonstration of feline love.

Within two to three days of birth, each kitten in a litter chooses his or her own teat, and from then on, generally only takes a nip from this nipple.

Q *Is it better to board a cat or get a pet sitter?*

A It depends on the cat. More cats would probably prefer to be looked in on a couple of times a day in their own familiar surroundings (same bed, same perch, same smells, same view) by a pet sitter, but there are also those cats who are adaptable enough to do well in a boarding situation.

Do be sure, though, that you get a backstage tour of any facility you're considering. Not too long ago, it wasn't uncommon for boarding kennels to maximize their use of space by putting cages for cats on top of dog runs. Not good! Cats should be in a separate room (preferably a separate county, but you can't have everything) from the dogs. For cats, dogs – strange, noisy, smelly dogs – really is a four-letter word.

One time when boarding would really be an advantage is if your cat has a chronic illness, such as diabetes. In such cases, you're better off boarding at your veterinarian's office, if that's an option.

You should also look into newer pet resorts in your area, where stainless-steel cat cages are a thing of the past. Rather, cat condos feature floor-to-ceiling windows, multilevel perches, indoor/outdoor access, plush beds and even TV (featuring fabulous feline DVDs, of course).

To find an experienced, professional pet sitter in your area, check out www.ukpetsitters.org.

Q Should cats be sedated for air travel?

A People always assume that animals should be tranquilized for a plane ride, but in fact, they're better off flying drug-free. That's because tranquilized pets may be calmer, but the medication puts them at a greater risk of dying in a cargo hold.

Medication or no medication, think twice about putting your cat in the cargo hold if he's a flat-faced breed, such as the Persian. These cats do not breathe well under ideal conditions, and a cargo hold isn't any cat's idea of ideal conditions. Especially when they're stressed!

Of course, if you're flying with your cat, he may not have to fly in the cargo hold. Some airlines, particularly American ones, allow a couple of small pets in the passenger cabin on each flight, as long as the animal's carrier will fit under the seat. They'll usually consider the pet one of your allowable pieces of carry-on luggage, and they'll charge you an outrageous fee besides. So it goes.

If you're taking your cat in the cabin as a carry-on pet, you may want to consider mild sedation after all. Talk to your veterinarian (or your own physician, depending on who you think will need the medication more). Or have a few more drinks and that squirming mass in the bag – once you quit fiddling and fussing over him – will probably calm right down.

Q *I've read that dogs have cat fleas. So, do cats have dog fleas?*

A Nope. Cats have cat fleas, although the pests like dogs just as well.

In 1834, a Frenchman by the name of Bouché took a flea off a cat, described it in the scientific literature and gave it the name Pulex felis (*felis* is Latin for cat). He actually got the first part, the genus, wrong, but he was the first to use felis as a species name for a flea. The Entomological Society gives all insects common names, so *Ctenocephalides felis* (with the correct genus) was officially named the cat flea.

Bouché could have taken the same flea species from a dog, fox or lynx in France, and today we might be calling it the dog, fox or lynx flea. There is a dog flea (*Ctenocephalides canis*), which, as you might suspect, was first described after its removal from a dog. However, this is a rare species and has seldom been caught in a flea comb in North America over the past twenty years. In most countries, the cat flea is the most common flea found on both dogs and cats.

There are about 500 different kinds of fleas, each named for their meal of preference. There's even a human flea!

Q *Why do cats chew on sweaters and blankets? Is there something missing in their diet?*

A This condition is called wool-sucking. (How long do you think it took some behaviorist to come up with that label?) Imagine being so afflicted and facing the backyard taunts from the neighbor cats, 'Sparky is a wool-sucker, Sparky is a wool-sucker!' Although it's especially common in Siamese and other Oriental breeds, it's certainly not uncommon in the general cat population.

No one is really sure what causes it, but it probably doesn't have anything to do with a dietary deficiency. More likely, it's one of those habits (like people who chew fingernails, pop knuckles or chew gum) that relieves stress and brings comfort.

The best we can offer is some 'might help, can't hurt' suggestions.

You should definitely put away anything that's too nice to be damaged, like Great-Grandma's quilt that won first place at the 1908 Iowa County Fair. Keep bedrooms off-limits by closing the doors, to protect the blankets on the beds.

Set out some 'decoy' blankets and apply a taste deterrent such as Bitter Apple, Tabasco or hot pepper oil. This might break the habit, but it might not. Spraying fabrics lightly with perfume is also a common recommendation.

Some experts believe that increasing the fiber in the cat's diet may also help. You can do that by regularly adding a little canned pumpkin – it's also good for hairballs. Just make sure it's the plain kind – no added sugar or spice. More activity is also recommended, such as playing with your cat regularly with a fishing pole-type toy or other lure object.

The term 'cat's pajamas' comes from an English tailor of the late 1700s and early 1800s who made the finest silk pajamas for royalty and other rich patrons. His name was E. B. Katz.

Q *How can I keep the neighbor's cat out of my yard?*

A Safe to say that 'Why won't my cat use the litter box?' is the top question cat lovers ask us. The top question everyone who doesn't have a cat asks is this one. And it's completely understandable. If you spend all day Saturday waxing your new car, you aren't too happy to come out Sunday morning to find muddy cat prints on the hood. If you're an avid gardener, you don't want your flowerbeds (and even less, your vegetable garden) turned into a cat's toilet.

Many people are pretty good-natured about this problem, figuring that cats have roamed since the beginning of time, will roam until the end of time, and that . . . um . . . stuff happens, to paraphrase a popular saying. Other folks are extremely intolerant of roaming cats, to the point of doing them harm or trapping them and dumping them at the nearest animal-control facility. (Another reason why keeping your cat indoors is an excellent idea.)

Is there a humane way to keep a cat out of your yard? We've never heard of anyone having much long-term luck with all the things people put in their gardens to discourage cats from loitering – and we've heard them all: pepper, citrus peels, and even the person now and then who insists that sprinkling a cup of his own urine around the perimeter will do the trick.

We think a lot of cats are laughing at that last one.

Putting sharp-edge decorative gravel in as ground cover will help, as will putting down mesh that plants can grow through but cats can't dig under.

One of the better options we've run across over the years is the motion-detector sprinkler. Any animal who trips the detector is immediately going to get sprayed with water. You can imagine how much a cat enjoys that. It's a reasonable solution, we think. Nobody gets hurt, the cat goes elsewhere and your lawn gets watered. Works pretty well on some other critters, too, such as foxes.

Q Can I put my cat in my will?

A You absolutely should. What you shouldn't do is leave all your worldly belongings to your cat. That's going to stand up in court for about one minute, and the vile nephew you never really liked or trusted will end up with everything and give your cat the boot.

We know you love your cat a lot more than that nephew, but it doesn't matter. In the eyes of the law, an animal is a piece of property with little more legal status than a chair. Instead, you must leave your pet (and money to take care of the animal, if you can) to a friend, relative or organization that will look out for your cat's interests for the rest of his life. Some states and the UK now recognize trusts to help you do exactly that, but of course, you should talk to a lawyer to find out what works best for you and your cat.

Q Why is a cat's tongue like sandpaper?

A If you look at a cat's tongue with a magnifying glass (and good luck trying to do that, by the way!), you'll see it's covered with row after row of barbs. For you scientific types, these little structures that line the surface of a cat's tongue are called filiform papillae. They're hooked (like the wiry half of Velcro) and are directed toward the throat.

These barbs help to hold prey while eating, and they also help a cat keep her fur in perfect (or should we say purrfect?) condition, pulling out dead and dying hairs along with any debris picked up in the day's travels. Cats can actually feel when a few hairs are out of place, so that tongue is also a convenient, built-in hairbrush.

It's the start of an assembly line for some mighty fine hairballs, as well. Since the hooks direct items down the throat – like an auger – it's difficult for cats to expel fur objects (or yarn, fishing line or other things that rightly ought to be expelled) from their mouths. This is one reason cats swallow rather than spit out fur, and then hack it up as hairballs.

Other papillae of the tongue are involved with taste detection. The filiform papillae can't taste food, but they do hold food in contact with the tongue long enough to enable the cat to taste it.

Cats can function with no teeth, but they must have at least half their tongue to survive.

Q *When a cat is clawing the furniture, is he sharpening his claws?*

A The result of scratching – whether repeated slashes on a bedpost or hieroglyphics on the corner of the couch – is sharp claws, but they don't get that way from being honed like a knife. When a cat is scratching, what she's really doing is removing the outer layer of worn-out claw sheaths. Underneath are sharp new claws.

If you look closely where your cat scratches, you'll probably find one of these old sheaths from time to time. They look like little silver crescent moons.

If the scratching post or the hieroglyphic art the cat draws on your sofa doesn't do the trick, cats will use their teeth to chew off the old outer casings.

Like the requisite warm-up for an aerobics or hair-obics class, scratching also helps a cat stretch out her spine (she anchors those front claws and then s-t-r-e-t-c-h-e-s) and mark a little territory with the visual aid of scratch marks and the scent pads in her feet.

Why do a cat's claws retract?

A You don't want studded snow tires in the middle of the summer, and you only engage four-wheel drive when you need it. Just as snow tires can slow a car down, a cat's claws can slow him down. So the cat retracts them in order to ambulate (a fancy way of saying walk) without continuously catching his claws. Cat claws come out only when they're needed.

It's a mistake to refer to claws as retractable, by the way. The normal, relaxed position of a cat's claw is retracted, or sheathed. To bring out those daggers, a cat must voluntarily contract muscles and rubber-band-like elastic ligaments underneath her toes. If it was the other way around, the poor cat would have to keep her muscles tensed all day long to keep her claws sheathed.

Q We got a cat to take care of the mice in the barn, but he barely seems interested. My uncle says we should stop feeding him so he gets hungry enough to eat fast food. Is that true?

A Withholding food doesn't motivate hunting, since the behavior is driven by instinct. A good hunter will do his job on a full tummy or an empty one. Catching and eating are two different things in a cat's mind.

The urge to chase and capture is instinctive, but the strength of that instinct varies from cat to cat. The cat's mom bestows on her kittens both a genetic heritage and early lessons on how to hunt successfully. Therefore, a kitten who is the progeny of a poor mouser is likely to be a poor mouser himself – even if you buy him a copy of *Mousing for Dummies*.

If you really need a cat who is the Verminator, go to farmers in your area and ask if they have any young mousers up for adoption. Be prepared to trap a cat who has not been properly socialized as a young kitten, and have the cat spayed or neutered. (It's a myth that this diminishes a cat's hunting instinct.) Then, confine the cat in your barn with food, clean water and a litter box for at least a week to establish a new home base. Continue to provide five-star service for a few weeks to keep the talent close to home.

Pamper these felines like the star athletes they are, and you will keep them gainfully employed in your arena.

Q What's a cat's top speed?

A The average domestic cat can run at a speed of around thirty miles per hour. Egyptian maus are reportedly the fastest breed of domestic cat, capable of reaching thirty-six miles per hour. The American shorthair is next, at thirty-one miles per hour.

To put things in perspective, the thoroughbred is the fastest breed of horse and can maintain a speed of forty-five miles per hour for over a mile. But it's a cat of a different color who is the fastest animal on land. The cheetah can run in bursts of seventy miles per hour.

Q Do cats get depressed?

A The emotional range of a cat is not all that wide or deep, to be honest. That's one reason why a cat who seems to show what, in humans, might be signs of depression – lethargy, loss of appetite and changes in normal sleep patterns – is more likely to have a physical problem than a mental one.

Still, there's no denying that many cat lovers have observed what looks a lot like grief in pets who have lost a family member, either four-legged or two-legged.

So, yes, it seems some cats do have an emotional response to the loss of a beloved person or pet they share their lives with.

But cats are also amazingly resilient when it comes to joining a new family. Think of shelter cats. Can you imagine how much time people would have to spend in therapy if they were suddenly removed from one family and placed with another – in some cases, again and again? Although some newly adopted cats go through an adjustment period that may include being anxious and hiding, most bounce back and become happy new family members.

'Love the one you're with,' seems to be the motto of many a cat.

For people suffering from depression, studies show that one of the best treatment plans is to get a pet. The companionship, the responsibility and even the increase in activity required are all good for lifting people out of depression, or preventing it in the first place.

Q Is it okay for my cat to eat dog food?

A No, it's not. Cats aren't dogs, and dogs aren't cats, and their nutritional requirements are quite different. Cats seem to instinctively know this, and most of them aren't all that interested in the dog's dinner. The opposite isn't true, by the way: A lot of dogs just love cat food, which isn't good for them, either. Both dogs and cats are hunters and carnivores, which means they eat meat. But dogs have a broader range of foods they can get nutrition from, because dogs can hunt and also scavenge for their meals. And when you're a scavenger, you pretty much take what you get. Cats, on the other hand, are what are called obligate carnivores. They cannot survive without the nutrients found in meat, and they require higher levels of protein in their diets than dogs do. (This is also why experts say that cats cannot be vegetarians.) Because of this, pet-food manufacturers have a different formula for making cat food than they use in making dog food. Don't let your pets nibble from each other's bowls, in other words. Oh sure, a little bit here and there won't hurt them, but to feed a cat a steady diet of dog food (or vice versa) is not conducive to long-term health.

A BETTER CAT FOOD

My Cats for Dummies coauthor and friend, veterinary cardiologist Dr Paul Pion, is credited with making a discovery that saves the lives of tens of thousands of cats a year. While a researcher at the University of California, Davis, Dr Pion discovered a link between taurine deficiency in commercial cat foods and the often fatal heart disease dilated cardiomyopathy. Because of Dr Pion's discovery, cat foods were reformulated. More than twenty years later, Dr Pion is now head of the Veterinary Information Network (VIN.com) and VeterinaryPartner.com, but the vanity plates on his car still note the important nutritional milestone: They say 'TAURINE.' Taurine, by the way, is one of those critical elements that cats get from eating meat.

— Gina Spadafori

Q *If cats are carnivores, why don't we just serve them bowls of meat every day?*

A What we think of as 'meat' — flesh and muscle — is only a part of the natural diet of a wild feline. In fact, wild felines also eat skin, bones, guts and even stomach contents of their prey. A pampered pet dining on nothing but sautéed chicken breast is not being well served – and would eventually become ill from malnutrition. As top veterinary cardiologist Dr Paul Pion is fond of saying, the perfect meal for a cat would be to put one whole, freshly killed mouse or other small rodent in a blender and hit 'purée.' Serve warm. Most of us aren't going to fix meals like this, no matter how much we love our cats. Some people do provide their cats with home-prepared meals, but to do this successfully requires more research, time and expense than most people can or are willing to commit. Generations of cats have lived long and healthy lives on commercial pet foods that combine multiple sources of protein, not just those made primarily from meat. If you're not sure how best to feed your cat, ask your veterinarian for specific recommendations.

Q Is declawing cats really such a bad idea?

A In answering this question, we show that we're brave enough (or foolish enough) to wade into the boiling-hot waters of controversy. Declawing isn't like cutting your nails or nipping the tips of your cat's claws. It's the surgical amputation under anesthesia of the last digit on each 'finger' of a cat's front paws. Picture cutting your fingers off at the first knuckle back from the end and you'll get an idea. Now do you see why this is so controversial? Many shelters and rescue groups refuse to place a cat or kitten with someone who won't sign a statement that he or she won't declaw. Some veterinarians refuse to perform the procedure, and some feline advocates argue that declawing makes a cat more likely to bite, less likely to use a litter box and harder to place in a new home if the animal ends up in a shelter. Others disagree on all these points. What cannot be argued is that declawing is painful and, in many cases, can be avoided with retraining techniques that teach a cat to use scratching posts to perform the natural and very satisfying scratching routines. We believe that declawing should never be the first option when it comes to dealing with a cat's furniture-scratching behavior, no matter how angry you are that the corners of your expensive new couch are in tatters. A quick search of the Internet, library or bookstore will provide you with information on how to train your cat to leave your furniture alone. (While retraining, putting double-sided tape on the sides of your furniture, or on a piece of cardboard mounted to the side of your furniture, will discourage your cat from scratching since cats hate putting their paws on sticky stuff.) In a perfect world, everyone would have the patience and the tolerance to retrain a furniture-clawing cat or live with the unwanted behavior. But the fact is that some otherwise good homes have people in them – such as an only marginally cat-tolerant spouse – who make clawing an issue and insist on declawing as a condition of the pet's staying. We may not like this fact, but we live with it. Better yet, we suggest that if you know you're going to be absolutely intolerant of a furniture-clawing cat, you adopt an adult cat who has already been declawed. If that's not possible, please try every strategy you can find to retrain your cat to use a scratching post before submitting her to this painful elective procedure.

THE GREAT DECLAWING DEBATE

How strongly do some people feel about declawing? So much so that I once had someone throw a drink in my face at a party when I admitted that I could see that in some cases — relatively few — declawing was a good option. And every time I've written about declawing for my syndicated newspaper column, I've been flooded with e-mails from both sides of the issue.

— Gina Spadafori

Q *Final question: Do you guys ever get tired of giving advice to pet lovers every day of your lives until the end of time?*

A Of course not! It's either do this or get real jobs. Not to mention, how many jobs can you have in this world where every single day you can make someone's life a little better, just by sharing your love of animals and your hard-earned knowledge of how to make living with them easier?

Not many, huh? Truth to tell, we consider ourselves lucky, and more than a little bit blessed.

And that, as they say, is our final answer.

Acknowledgments

This book, and its canine companion volume, would not have been possible without the generosity of the many top veterinarians, behaviorists and other experts who were gracious and generous in providing their expertise. It's exciting and inspiring to us to know and be able to share ideas with such an outstanding group of professionals – brilliant and caring people who have dedicated their careers to improving the lives of pets and the people who love them.

We both owe so much to Marty's colleague, Dr Rolan Tripp of AnimalBehavior.net, and his wife, Susan, for their keen and expert eyes on this project, their injections of creativity, and their help in making everything good even better.

Our gratitude also goes out to all the veterinarians who helped us. We especially want to thank Dr Jan Bellows, companion animal dental specialist at All Pets Dental Clinic in Pembroke Pines, Florida; Dr Gilbert Burns, associate professor of anatomy at Washington State University College of Veterinary Medicine (who knows as much as anyone in history about feline genitalia); Dr Tom Catanzaro, international veterinary consultant and author of twelve books; Dr Nicholas Dodman, head of the Animal Behavior Department at the Cummings School of Veterinary Medicine at Tufts University; Dr Keven P. Gulikers of the Animal Referral and Emergency Center of Arizona in Mesa, Arizona; Dr Kim Kendall, board-certified animal behavior expert and owner of the Cat Clinic of Sydney, Australia; Dr Kyle Kerstetter, chief of surgery at Michigan Veterinary Specialists near Detroit, Michigan; Dr Stephanie Lifton, a board-certified specialist in internal medicine; Dr Susan Little, president of Winn Feline Foundation; Dr Gary Norsworthy of the Alamo Feline Health Center in San Antonio, Texas; Dr Will Novak, chief medical officer of Banfield, the Pet Hospital; Dr Paul Pion of the Veterinary Information Network and VeterinaryPartner.com, a board-certified veterinary cardiologist; Dr Christopher Pagel, owner of the Companion Animal Hospital in Madison, Wisconsin, and A Behavior Vet for Cats (www.catdoc.biz); Dr Arnold Plotnick, board-certified specialist in internal medicine at Manhattan Cat Specialists in New York; Dr James Richards, director of the Cornell Feline Health Center, past president of the American Association of Feline Practitioners and author of The ASPCA Complete Guide to Cats; Dr Samuel Vainisi of Denmark, Wisconsin, a board-certified specialist in ophthalmology; Dr Drew Weigner of thecatdoctoratlanta.com, feline specialist and past president of Academy Feline Medicine; Dr Janice Willard of Moscow, Idaho; and Dr Sandy Writer, an internal medicine specialist and consultant with Antech Diagnostics.

On a more personal level, we simply cannot do what we do without the support of our family and friends.

For Marty, two-legged family includes his beloved wife, Teresa (a gifted writer in her own right), daughter, Mikkel, and son, Lex. Not to mention the four-legged family members – dogs, cats and horses – on the Becker family's Almost Heaven Ranch in northern Idaho. Worthy of special recognition is his colleague, friend and mentor, Dr Scott Campbell, the founder, CEO and chairman of the board of Banfield, The Pet Hospital.

For Gina, two-legged family starts with her brother Joe, who is also one of her very best friends. Always, too, there's the support of her parents, Louise and Nino, fifty-two years married and still going strong, and her brother Pete, his wife, Sally, and their bright and talented children, Kate and Steven. This book would not have been possible without the help of Gina's community of friends, colleagues and pet lovers, especially Dr Signe Beebe, Judithanne Bloom, Melinie DiLuck, Jan Haag, Sonia Hansen, Don Linville, Christie Keith, Scott Mackey, John McDonald, Greg Melvin, Morgan Ong, Dr Bill Porte, Dick Schmidt, Monica Siewert and Mary Young. And of course, the pet residents of the northern California home Gina is now calling the Almost Crazy Ranch.

Thanks from us both to the folks at Health Communications, Inc., especially Peter Vegso, who saw the promise of this book and its canine companion volume and gave us the go-ahead to write together and have a great time doing so. We'd also like to note in appreciation and heartfelt respect the work of our editors, Allison Janse and Beth Adelman.

– Dr Marty Becker, drmartybecker.com

– Gina Spadafori, petconnection.com

We know you have more than 101 questions about your cat! So we're already planning another book to answer even more of your questions.